GET STARTED

The Beginner's Guide to *Computers*

David McCormick

GEDDES & GROSSET

Trademarks

Thank you to Google and to Yahoo! for the use of their logos and for permission to reproduce screenshots of their web pages in this book.

Microsoft, MSN, Outlook Express, Hotmail, Excel, Word, Windows and Windows XP are all trademarks of the Microsoft Corporation whom we thank for the use of their logos and for desktop screenshots.

All other brand or product names used in this book are recognised as trademarks or registered trademarks of their respective companies.

Published 2005 by Geddes & Grosset, David Dale House, New Lanark, ML11 9DJ

Text by David McCormick
Illustrations by Mike Fuller
Cover design by Mark Mechan

ISBN 1 84205 426 0

Printed and bound in Poland

POLSKABOOK

Contents

Introduction

Computers are all around us. They are used in airports to track passengers and their baggage, in hospitals as part of sophisticated scanning devices, in schools and colleges to assist learning and in the home they can be used for a wide range of activities from playing games to calculating a household budget.

They also come in all shapes and sizes. The original computers filled whole rooms and some still do – in fact, the Earth Simulator computer in Tokyo takes up an area about half the size of a football pitch! Others are tiny and fit into household items such as microwaves and fridges. You can even buy a fridge which uses an embedded computer to order up more food over the Internet when supplies are running low! However, this book is concerned with the more common PC desktop and laptop or notebook computers that can be bought in the high street and used in the home.

Desktop computers like the one in the diagram on page 10 can be quite bulky and take up a lot of desk space. Slimmer screens which use liquid crystal displays (LCD), such as those used in calculators, are now available at more competitive prices which can help if you have restricted space in which to set up a computer.

Laptops and notebooks offer a portable alternative to desktops but they are more expensive, cost more to repair and are harder to upgrade should you need a faster machine two years from now.

Fig. I.1 Laptop and desktop computers

PCs and Macs

Computer stores stock two different classes of computer – PCs (Personal Computers) which are made by a range of manufacturers and Macs (or, more fully, Macintoshes) which are made by Apple. PCs are sometimes also referred to as being IBM compatible. Macs are quite different technically to PCs and anything you buy for a Mac will probably not work on a PC and likewise the other way round.

Macs were originally a lot easier to use than PCs because you controlled them through small pictures (known as **icons)** on the computer screen rather than with seemingly obscure codes and symbols which the original PCs used. Today's PCs now also use the same graphical (pictorial) approach as Macs.

Macs have proved very popular with those who work in visually creative jobs such as graphic design or advertising.

The machines themselves have very distinctive screens and cases and make most PCs look decidedly boring. However, PCs are much more popular because they are generally cheaper than Macs and there is usually a wider range of software such as games or business programs available.

This book focuses entirely on PC equipment running Microsoft software. Chapter 1 looks at the different hardware components – the keyboard, monitor, mouse, etc. that make up a computer then Chapter 2 looks at system software – the programs through which you control your machine.

Chapter 3 covers how to use your computer: from switching on and using your mouse for the first time to the use of files and folders to store your work. The chapter concludes with a section on computer maintenance.

Chapters 4 and 5 cover Word – Microsoft's program for word processing. Word is the program that is covered in most detail here because word processing is often the first computer application that most people learn and it is one of the most useful. In addition, Microsoft's programs have many features in common so that once you have learned them in Word you will recognise them later when you begin to use Excel or Internet Explorer.

Chapter 6 is an introduction to Excel and provides sufficient background to enable first-time users to build a basic spreadsheet for a household budget and to represent it as a chart.

Chapter 7 looks at the Internet and in particular the World Wide Web. How to use Internet Explorer is covered and there are guidelines on choosing an Internet service provider.

Chapter 8 covers Outlook Express – how to send and receive email messages, and how to attach and handle files. There are also sections on 'netiquette' and on 'spam'.

Chapter 9 covers safe use of your computer when online. It covers antivirus programs and firewalls and there are guidelines for safer 'surfing'.

Chapter 10 is a brief overview of some of the features available within Windows that make computers more accessible for people who have a visual impairment or have difficulty when using a hand-held device such as a computer mouse.

The book finishes with a short glossary of common computer terms.

Chapter 1
Hardware

A computer needs both hardware and software to work. **Hardware** is all the equipment such as the screen, the keyboard and the electronic circuits inside the computer box. **Software** is the word used for the instructions or **programs** which control the hardware and allow it to work as a computer. This chapter covers the key hardware components of your computer while Chapter 2 introduces the main types of software.

A desktop computer usually consists of a box and several peripheral items of hardware such as a monitor (the screen), a keyboard and a mouse (a pointing device). The term **'peripheral'** is often used to refer to anything outside the box and includes things like printers, loudspeakers, scanners and joysticks for games.

Fig. 1.1 System unit and peripherals

A peripheral allows you to communicate with your computer. There are two types: those which provide **input** and enable you to tell the computer what you want it to do (such as the keyboard and mouse) and those which display **output** such as the monitor or printer.

Input

The keyboard

The keyboard is one of the main ways in which you will send instructions and data to your computer. It has several types of key. There are letter, number and punctuation keys which are similar to those of a typewriter – holding down **Shift** while keying a letter gives you a capital, while pressing **Enter** (Return) starts a new paragraph.

Along the top of the keyboard are **function keys** (F1-F12) which do different things in different programs but F1 is usually a link to the Help facility.

There are also **navigational** or **arrow keys** to help you move around the screen, a **numeric keypad** to make it easier when you are keying in figures, and various special keys such as Control, Alt and the Windows keys.

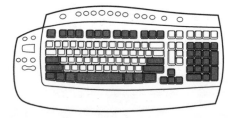

Fig. 1.2 A standard keyboard with main key types highlighted

If you have not used a keyboard before you may find that if you press a key and do not release it within 0.5 second several copies of the letter or number that you pressed appear on the screen. The computer interprets the held-down key as repeated key strokes. If after some practice you find that this continues to be a problem you can adjust your computer's settings to ignore repeated keystrokes over a longer period (see Chapter 10 on Accessibility).

The mouse

The other main way in which you will control your computer is through your mouse. If you place a mouse on a flat surface and move it to the side a pointer on the screen also moves to the side. The mouse allows you to move quickly to any point on the screen so that you can make changes to text, or select options from an onscreen list, or open a program. You communicate your choices to the computer by clicking (quickly pressing) a button on the mouse. How to use the mouse is covered in Chapter 3 Using Your Computer.

Fig. 1.3 Standard mouse

Mice (or mouses, both are acceptable usage)come in all shapes and sizes. A typical mouse has a roller ball underneath to enable it to move smoothly in any direction when in use, has a cable connecting it to the computer and has a left and a right button to click. However, you can also buy cordless mice which work using infrared light like a TV remote control and optical mice which work without a roller ball. (A roller ball can pick up dirt which then affects the operation of the mouse.)

Other ways to point

Touchpads are touch-sensitive areas that are often found built into the keyboards of laptop computers. You move your finger over the touchpad to move the pointer on the screen and there are buttons alongside to click.

A **trackball** is another pointing device often built in to laptops. The trackball is in effect an inverted mouse – you roll the ball with your hand.

Other input devices

Digital cameras, scanners and microphones are also examples of input devices. When you take a picture with a digital camera it converts the light which enters the lens into a pattern of digital electrical signals. This pattern is then stored in the memory card of the camera. The camera becomes an input device when you subsequently connect it to a computer to download your pictures for editing and printing.

A **scanner** can be used in several ways when connected to a computer as an input device. When you scan something on a flatbed scanner, the sensor moves progressively across the item being scanned (like a photocopier), picks up the image and converts it into electrical signals (like a digital camera) which are then input to the computer for processing.

A scanner can be used to convert conventionally printed photographs into digital form so that you can store them on your computer, edit them or email them to a friend. In combination with **optical character recognition** (**OCR**) software, a scanner can also be used to copy and convert text from a printed document so that it can be amended in a word processing program such as Microsoft Word. However, the most straightforward use of a scanner is probably as a form of photocopier.

A microphone becomes an input device when used in conjunction with a **speech recognition program** that will enable you to dictate text rather than type it or to use voice commands rather than clicking with the mouse.

The System Unit

This box contains several key parts of your computer system including the main system board (also known as the motherboard), the microprocessor (also known as the CPU – central processing unit), the computer's memory and its disk storage.

Microprocessor

The **microprocessor** is the 'brain' of your computer and looks like this.

Fig. 1.4 Microprocessor

It is here that the input from the keyboard and mouse is eventually sent and where the program instructions are implemented. It can process billions of instructions per second and organises the traffic of electronic signals throughout the computer such as directing information to the screen, to the printer or to a disk for storage.

Although it processes billions of instructions every second the processor can only carry out one procedure at a time. It has a timeslot in which to carry out each operation which is controlled by a clock. The faster the clock 'ticks', the faster the processor works and the better the performance of the computer. This clock rate is measured in megahertz (MHz) or gigahertz (GHz) and is often quoted in the advertising for a computer. A 2.5 Gigahertz microprocessor can process up to 2,500,000,000 instructions per second.

However, if you buy a computer with a 3 GHz processor it doesn't mean that it will be twice as fast as one with a 1.5 GHz chip. The speed of the computer is ultimately determined by how fast the input, output and storage hardware can work.

Disk storage

Your computer stores its programs and any files that you have created on its **hard disk**. This is the main storage area for the computer and it works rather like an audio cassette tape in that it records information on a surface that can be magnetised.

There are actually many disks within a hard disk drive and like an audio cassette there are read/write heads which either 'play back' or record information on the disk. To cover the disk surface the disk drive spins the disks and the read/write heads move out and in. Each disk usually has at least two read/write heads as shown in the diagram.

Fig. 1.5 Hard disk drive

The smallest piece of information that can be stored is called a **bit** and it can be a 1 or 0. The bits are usually handled by the computer in groups of eight, sixteen or thirty two. A group of eight bits is known as a **byte** and a **kilobyte** is 1024 bytes. The reason it is not exactly 1000 bytes is because the simplest way for a computer manufacturer to increase the size of a storage area is to double it. So starting with 8 bytes and then multiplying by two we get:

$$8 \times 2 = 16$$
$$16 \times 2 = 32$$
$$32 \times 2 = 64$$
$$64 \times 2 = 128$$
$$128 \times 2 = 256$$
$$256 \times 2 = 512$$
$$512 \times 2 = \mathbf{1024}$$

So a kilobyte of storage actually contains 1024 bytes.

In the same way, a **megabyte** is roughly 1 million bytes (actually 1,048,576) and a **gigabyte** is approximately 1000 million bytes. So a 40 GB hard drive will hold about 340,000,000,000 bytes.

Hard disks are usually built into computers so if you want to move something you have been working on to another machine, or don't want to fill your hard disk with data that you will only use infrequently, what options are there?

Floppy disks work on the same principle as hard disks in that they store information by magnetising the surface of a disk. They hold a lot less information (typically 1.4 MB) but they can be removed from the computer to let you exchange information with others or to keep back-up copies for security reasons.

The floppy disk is a thin circle of plastic which is protected by a square plastic case. The plastic case has a metal shutter which slides to the side to expose the disk surface when the disk is inserted in the disk drive. If this shutter becomes bent or damaged in anyway it is best to throw it away as it could let dirt onto the disk surface – or stick in your disk drive!

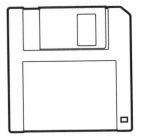

Fig. 1.6 Floppy disk

In one corner of the floppy disk is a small square sliding mechanism. Slide this switch so that a hole appears if you want to **write-protect** a disk so that it cannot be overwritten.

If you bought a new program in the 1980s and 1990s it would be supplied on several floppy disks – possibly six or more! Today, programs are sold on CD-ROMs or DVDs because they hold much more information – 650 Megabytes in the case of a CD-ROM and up to 5 Gigabytes on a DVD.

CD-ROM stands for **compact disc – read-only memory** which means that the disk is like an audio CD that you can play music from but you cannot record anything new on it. If you want to store large files or amounts of data that will not fit on a floppy disk you need to use a CD-R (**compact disc – recordable**) with an appropriate CD-writer drive and associated program. These have 300 times the storage capacity of a floppy disk but you can only 'write' to them once. If you want to be able to write to a CD more than once, you need CD-RW (**compact disc – rewritable**) hardware.

CD-ROM drive speeds are often quoted in the

specifications for computer. A speed of 24x indicates a drive that reads data 24 times faster than an audio CD.

A DVD provides much more storage capacity than a CD-ROM and will easily store video files. It is for this reason that DVD has become regarded as standing for Digital Video Disc – although it was originally intended to be called Digital Versatile Disc.

Main memory

The microprocessor can read from or write to a hard disk within a few thousandths of a second but the processor can handle billions of instructions per second. Another form of memory is needed to make the most of the speed of the processor.

Random Access Memory (RAM) is the **main memory** of the computer and is where the CPU keeps the programs and data that are being worked on. It is much faster than disk storage because it has no moving parts. It is entirely electronic and looks like a grid of small micro-processors. However, it differs from other forms of storage in that when the computer is switched off anything held in the memory is lost. Modern desktop computers generally have either 256 or 512 megabytes of RAM.

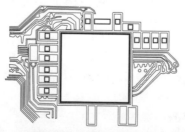

Fig. 1.7 RAM chips on a SIMM or DIMM card

Read Only Memory (ROM) is another type of memory that is chip based. In this case the contents of the memory are not lost when the computer closes down but you also cannot change what is in the memory – it is read-only. These features make ROM the ideal place to store the boot program which starts your computer.

What happens when you start your computer and a program is run

When you switch on your computer the system carries out a POST (Power On Self Test). The start-up sequence or boot sequence is then triggered to locate the system software on the hard disk and it is copied into RAM. Working within the system software, a program such as Microsoft Word is selected. The CPU requests the program from the hard disk and it too is copied into RAM. You see the program on screen and start using it. Any data that you input is also held in RAM until you save or close the file when it is automatically placed on the hard disk. When you close the program the space that it took up in RAM can be overwritten or used by another application. The program does not need to be returned to the hard disk because it was copied from there initially. The system software remains in RAM until the computer is shut down.

Other internal hardware

Video adapter

It is the video adapter or graphics card that supports the

link between the CPU and the monitor. It may be part of the **mother board** which holds the microprocessor and other key components or it may be an upgradeable graphics card that fits into an expansion slot. (The latest video cards require a special **Accelerated Graphics Port (AGP)** slot.) A graphics card has its own processor and memory. The faster the processor and the larger the memory, the better the card will be at handling video and computer games. Some cards offer features such as an integrated TV tuner, so you can add an aerial and watch television, or another monitor so you can work across two screens as if they were one.

Sound card

The sound card manages the audio output of your computer taking digital signals made up of a stream of 1's and 0's from the CPU and converting them to analogue wave signals for the loudspeakers to then convert into sound.

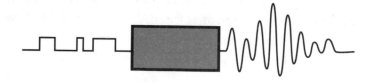

Fig. 1.8 Digital signal converted into an analogue signal

The sound card enables a range of leisure activities such as listening to music CDs, watching videos on DVD, playing games or listening to Internet radio. Using a sound card with a **MIDI (Musical Instrument Digital Interface)** port, musicians can connect an electronic keyboard or drums and record their compositions on hard disk.

Adding a microphone and using the speech recognition software that is part of Windows (or purchasing a proprietary package) frees you to some extent from using the keyboard, while the ability to play back text in a spoken voice (text to speech or TTS) is also made possible by the sound card.

Modem

A dial-up **modem** enables you to connect your computer to a phone line so that you can send and receive emails or surf the World Wide Web. When you send an email the modem converts the digital output of the computer into analogue form so that it behaves like sound and can be transmitted down the phone line. This is known as *mod*ulation. When you receive an email the modem works in reverse converting the analogue signal that arrives into digital form that the computer can interpret. This is known as *dem*odulation.

Most computers now have modems built into them when they are manufactured. They fit into an expansion slot like a sound card or graphics card.

Dial-up modems can transfer data at a speed of up to 56 kilobits per second (kbs) which is fine for straightforward email messages but will seem quite slow for Internet use if you frequently visit web sites that use a lot of graphics or animation (see cable modems).

Cable modems

If you subscribe to cable TV you will probably be used to regular mailshots advertising the benefits of broadband Internet. The cable that carries the TV signal into your home can also be used to provide fast Internet access via a **cable modem**. Part of the available **bandwidth** which carries the TV channels is used to transmit the signals back and forth between your computer and the computers that support the cable company's Internet service. A cable modem differs from a dial-up modem in that it does not actually have to convert your computer's digital signals into analogue signals for transmission over the cable network – it is digital all the way, but it is still called a modem!

Imagine a cable company offers three different broadband speeds: 150 kbps, 600 kbps and 1024 kbps. If you opted for the 600 kb/s service you would find that a web page that took 18 seconds to download on a dial-up service would now download in only 2 seconds.

However, because cable suppliers expect users to mostly download (receive) content, their systems are not usually as fast at sending data from your computer to the Internet. Such 'asymmetric' connections are a lot less fast at uploading compared to downloading.

In addition, you may have to share part of your bandwidth with any neighbours who also subscribe to the cable service which may also reduce the speed of your connection. Try to find out about the **contention ratio** before you sign on the dotted line. A contention ratio of 10 users to 1 'connection' is a lot better than 50:1. (See chapter 7 for more information on Internet access.)

If you live in an area that does not have cable you may still be able to receive broadband through an **ADSL**

(Asymmetric Digital Subscriber Line) service from BT or other provider. ADSL uses the telephone network but operates over a much wider range of frequencies than a standard telephone connection. It is therefore able to use a large part of this bandwidth for Internet access.

Output devices

Monitor

Your screen, or **monitor**, is likely to be your most frequently used output device so if you intend to spend many hours using your computer and want to avoid a headache (literally!) it is worthwhile obtaining a good one that is clear to read, doesn't flicker and has no glare.

There are two main types of monitor available – the more traditional TV type of monitor and the newer thin, flat screens or **flat panel displays**.

Traditional monitors

The key part in a traditional monitor is the cathode ray tube (CRT). This sends a beam of electrons to the back of the screen which is covered in dots called phosphors that glow when the electrons strike them. To create an image, the beam is first directed to a corner at the top of the screen and then sweeps horizontally across to the other side. It next drops down a line and again sweeps across the screen. It continues to do this until it has covered the screen when it then goes back to the top and starts over again. All this happens many times a second and creates the impression of an image on the screen.

This explanation of how a screen works is for a black and white screen. Colour screens work in the same way but have three phosphors (a red, a blue and a green) for every dot on a monochrome screen and usually require three beams of electrons. By illuminating the red, green and blue phosphors by different amounts a full spectrum of colours can be obtained for every **pixel** (picture element) on the screen.

Fig. 1.9 A pixellated image

The **resolution** of a screen is the number of pixels that make up the screen image. It is usually expressed in the form 800 x 600 which means 800 pixels across the screen and 600 up and down. You can usually increase or decrease the resolution of your screen by set amounts. If you increase the resolution from say 800 x 600 to 1024 x 768 you will find that you can see more on screen at one time but that everything is slightly smaller. If you reduce the resolution to say 640 x 480 you will see less on screen but everything will be increased in size. Changing screen resolution is covered in Chapter 3.

Screen size is usually quoted in inches and is the length of a diagonal across the screen. Manufacturers sometimes quote screen sizes without taking into account the plastic casing round the monitor which often covers part of the screen and reduces the available area. You may find if you measure the size of your screen along the diagonal that it is less than the advertised size by as much as an inch. Look for the **viewable image size** if you want to know how big your screen is for practical purposes.

Dot pitch is the distance between neighbouring phosphor dots of the same colour. The smaller the dot pitch the sharper the image you will see on screen. The dot pitch for a good screen will be around 0.25 millimetres.

The number of times each second that the electron beam covers the screen from top to bottom is known as the **refresh rate.** The higher the figure for the refresh rate, the less the screen will flicker. A refresh rate of 60-70 Hertz (cycles per second) at the chosen resolution is recommended.

Flat panel monitors

Flat panel monitors or **liquid crystal displays (LCD)** use liquid crystal technology similar to that found in calculators. If you are thinking of buying a flat panel monitor look for one that uses **Thin Film Transistor (TFT)** technology – particularly if two or more people are ever likely to be viewing the screen at the same time. This is because flat panel displays can have a limited viewing angle. They are fine when you look at them straight on but if you move to the side the colours can change and they become difficult to read. The best TFT displays have a viewing angle of 170° vertically and horizontally virtually eliminating this problem.

Flat panel monitors are also affected by the time it takes

for the transistors to switch on and off. This is known as **rise and fall time** and produces a lag effect when you try to move an onscreen object by dragging it with the mouse – the object 'judders' across the screen rather than moving smoothly. The best flat screens have rise and fall times of around 15 milliseconds but even this may not be good enough for some games programs.

Compared to traditional CRT monitors, flat screens are usually brighter, have better contrast, weigh less, require less desk space and use about half the power. On the other hand, they can cost twice as much, can have limited viewing angles and do not display video very well.

Printers

The most popular types of printer for the home user are laser printers and inkjet printers.

Laser printers

Laser printers work like photocopiers. A laser is used to produce a pattern of dots of electrical charge on a metal roller with the pattern of electrical charge corresponding to the image of the page that is to be printed. The charged roller attracts toner powder which sticks to the dots. The roller next transfers the toner to a sheet of paper which is then heated to fix the toner and the printed page appears in the output tray.

As with monitors, the quality of a printer is partly measured by its resolution but in this case the resolution indicates the number of printed dots that could be used to produce an image. A typical resolution for a home-use laser printer would be 300 dots per inch (dpi) which is fine for printing correspondence but not ideal for printing photos.

Inkjet printers

An inkjet printer sprays ink onto paper through a print head that consists of tiny holes. The head moves back and forth across the page, printing one line at a time.

Laser or inkjet?

Laser and inkjet printers provide the home user with a range of options, benefits and drawbacks. Here are four key criteria that you would probably want to take into account when considering whether to buy a colour inkjet, a monochrome laser or a colour laser printer.

Cost

Inkjets are much cheaper to buy than laser printers. However, don't forget running costs. A typical inkjet replacement colour cartridge costs about £25 compared to £50 for a laser cartridge but over the long term laser costs per printed page are much less.

You can save money with an inkjet by refilling your ink cartridges or using recycled cartridges but see the comment below under Quality.

If you choose an inkjet make sure to opt for one with separate black and colour cartridges if you are likely to do a lot of black-only printing.

Speed

Laser printers are generally faster than inkjets. A personal laser will produce up to 20 pages per minute (ppm) compared with 10 pages per minute for a budget inkjet (on draft setting). However, some good general purpose inkjets do now claim print speeds of up to 20 ppm.

Quality

Lasers are best for printing text and really sharp line images. Inkjet printouts sometimes have a slightly fuzzy appearance to printed text as a result of the ink spreading into the paper fibres before it dries. The quality of the paper used is also a factor here.

If you use refilled cartridges you run the risk that the ink will not be of as good a quality as the original and that the nozzles which spray the ink will become blocked. Some printers will clean the nozzles for you so make sure that you have this facility on your printer if you intend to refill your cartridges.

Convenience

Inkjets win on convenience. They are smaller than lasers, print acceptable text for most everyday purposes and will even print reasonable photographs on photographic paper – although it may take 20 minutes to produce one page!

Photo printers

Some photoprinters use the best available inkjet components to produce prints with resolutions of around 2880 x 1440 dpi that rival quality traditional photographic prints. However, the quality comes at a price – expect to pay over £300 and don't assume that they will print A4 paper.

Loudspeakers

Finally, loudspeakers or headphones are essential output devices if you use your computer to play or record music, use multimedia programs or use voice recognition software.

Chapter 2
Software

The instructions or **programs** which enable the computer to produce something useful are known as **software**. There are two main kinds of software: system software and applications software.

System software

The **system software** (or **operating system**) controls the different parts of hardware which make up the computer system. It controls the order in which things happen and when things happen. It also maintains a list of the documents that you create and where they are stored on the computer's hard disk.

Microsoft's latest system software is called Windows XP. Previous versions of Windows for home users include Windows Millennium Edition, Windows 98 and Windows 95. Most of what is covered in this book can be carried out using the older versions of Windows but if you are using an older version your screen may look different to the screenshots shown here.

You may hear Windows being described as having a **graphical user interface** (GUI). This is referring to the use of small pictures called **icons** to represent programs, files or hardware. Clicking on a program icon using a mouse will start or **open** the program in a **window** which is a 'frame' that you work in. If you then open a second program it opens in a different window.

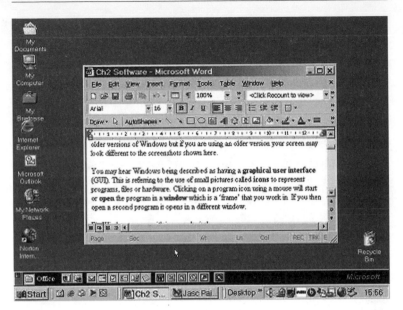

Fig. 2.1 Window open on desktop

Applications software

Applications software allows you to carry out what you want to do with the computer: word process, send email or surf the Internet. The Microsoft suite of programs has many common features making it easier to learn new programs after you have mastered the first.

You can use a **word processing** program like Microsoft Works Word to:

- write a letter
- prepare a newsletter for a club
- design an invitation for a party
- compile a cv to apply for a job
- prepare an advert to place in a newspaper
- design a poster for a garage clearance sale...

35

Word lets you correct mistakes, change your text as often as you want, move chunks of text without retyping them, add pictures, enlarge type, change typestyles. It will also check your spelling and grammar and tell you how many words you have written!

Where a word processor processes words, a **spreadsheet** processes numbers. Ever wondered where all your money goes each month? You can use Microsoft Works Spreadsheet or Microsoft Excel to keep track of your household budget or savings. They will even convert tables of numbers into graphs and charts to help you spot trends and patterns more easily.

Each letter that you write or spreadsheet that you create is known as a **document** and is stored as a **file** on your computer.

Email is one of the cheapest and quickest ways to keep in contact with friends and relatives all over the world. Outlook Express is an email program from Microsoft that enables you to compose and send emails and then to manage and store your incoming messages.

Outlook Express allows you to send more than simple text messages. You can **attach** documents such as Word files, Excel files or photographs to your emails.

Internet Explorer is Microsoft's **browser** program which you can use to 'surf' the World Wide Web. Use it to find out the latest news, to study or learn, to shop online or to book a holiday.

Two other Microsoft programs that you may hear about but which are not covered in this book are Access and PowerPoint. Access is Microsoft's powerful **database** program. A database is a collection of facts that are related to one another and which are organised in a particular way (such as a railway timetable). You could use a database to finally list that CD collection for insurance purposes or to build your definitive address book. PowerPoint is Microsoft's software for use in presentations. It is mostly used for business and so is not covered here.

Utility programs

Utility programs are a third category of program which carry out very specific tasks often connected to system management. For example, programs which help with disk maintenance or those which help you uninstall old programs that you no longer require.

Viruses

Computer **viruses** are also a form of software. They are programs which are intended to disrupt the working of your computer and the worst examples can cause havoc including possibly the loss of all your files. They can enter your computer from a CD or floppy disk which has been infected or via an email attachment or from programs downloaded from the internet.

Viruses are also often able to produce copies of themselves that are then sent to everyone in your email address book. It is therefore important to install an antivirus program such as McAfee VirusScan or Norton AntiVirus that will automatically scan all the email messages that you receive. You should also run your antivirus program each time you insert a disk into your computer that has been in someone else's machine.

In addition to an antivirus program it is important to

install a **firewall** to prevent hackers getting access to your machine when you go online. A firewall can either be hardware or software but most home users with a single machine use a software firewall. Windows XP includes a built in firewall but if you don't have windows XP you can purchase a suitable firewall from most computer shops or download one for free from the Internet.

Once you have installed a firewall and an antivirus program you need to keep them up to date. This is important because new viruses are constantly being created.

There is more information about antivirus and firewall protection in Chapter 9 which covers computer security.

Software bugs

It is not feasible to test a program for every eventuality so sometimes programming glitches get through which in certain circumstances can cause the computer to 'freeze' so that nothing works. These software problems are known as **bugs** and there is little you can do about them other than closing down the program or restarting your computer.

Copyright

Software is protected by copyright law. When you buy a program you are purchasing a licence to use it – you don't own the program. Under the terms of the licence you usually have to agree to use the program in certain ways, such as only installing it on one computer and not distributing copies to other people. If you install software on your computer for which you are not covered by a licence then you could be breaking the law.

There is software available that is free to use. Such

freeware is often found on CDs that are supplied with computer magazines. The copyright owner grants you the right to use such software for free but it will still have terms of use.

Shareware is similar to freeware in that you are free to use the software without charge for a limited period. Sometimes the owner simply asks you to send what you can by means of payment if you like the program.

Chapter 3
Using Your Computer

Switching on

When you power up (switch on) your computer the first thing it does is look for instructions about what to do. It finds these in its **boot loader** program. The term 'boot' is from the phrase 'to pull yourself up by the bootstraps' and this, in effect, is what the computer does.

The white-on-black text that you may see flashing across the screen as the computer boots is a test to check that everything is working. Once the self-test is complete it looks for the Windows operating system.

The first place it checks is in the floppy disk drive (drive a:) then it looks in the hard drive (usually drive c:). This is why if you ever inadvertently leave a floppy disk in the drive at the end of a work session you will see an error message saying that you have an invalid system disk when you next 'boot' your computer. Don't panic! Just remove the floppy and everything should be OK.

Once Windows is found it is loaded into memory and you see a Starting Windows message onscreen. You may see a screen asking for your user name and password – particularly if you are on a network in an office, library or Internet café.

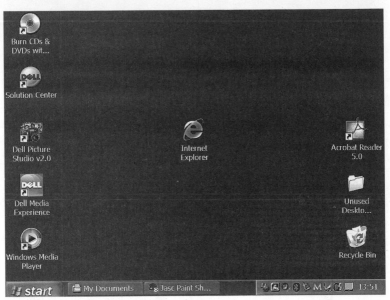

Fig. 3.1 Windows desktop with icons

Using a mouse for the first time

If you have never used a mouse before, try working through the instructions in this section. It covers the main aspects of using a mouse.

Start by placing the mouse on a mouse mat with the cable running away from you. Next, move the mouse from left to right and backwards and forwards while watching the screen. The outline arrowhead pointer follows your hand movements. Notice that the pointer can disappear off the edge of the screen but that it is only just off the edge and quickly comes back into view when you move the mouse back.

If you ever find that you are at the edge of your mouse mat and want to reposition the mouse, just lift it and move it to your preferred position. The pointer will not move when the roller ball in the mouse is not in contact with a hard surface (and likewise if you are using an optical mouse).

Pointing

The screen which you see when your computer finishes its starting up procedure is called the **desktop**. Use the mouse to explore any icons present on the desktop. Move the mouse so that is positioned over an icon and a short description of what the icon represents should appear. Moving the mouse over an icon in this way is known as **hovering** while the description that appears is called a **screen tip**. If you don't see any icons move the mouse down to the bottom left corner of the screen and the Start menu button should appear together with a screen tip like 'Click here to begin'.

Fig. 3.2 Screen tip of a desktop icon

Clicking

Don't click the Start button just yet but move the mouse to the centre of the screen and **right click** (press and release the right-hand button quickly). A pop-up menu appears. Move the mouse down the menu to **New**. A further menu should appear which includes the word Folder. Move the mouse onto Folder and **left click** (press and release the left-hand button quickly). A folder icon called

New Folder should appear on your desktop. It is in folders like these that you will place the files that you create when you write letters or emails.

Fig. 3.3 Folder icon

The menu which appears when you right click is known as a **context menu** because the items listed in it depend on the actions that you have recently carried out.

Clicking and dragging

Try **clicking-and-dragging** the new folder across the desktop. Move the mouse over the folder icon and left click. This **selects** the folder and the colour of the icon changes. Next, with the mouse over the new folder, left click but keep the button held down and move the mouse so that the new folder is dragged to another part of the screen then let go the button. Practice clicking and dragging the folder around the screen until you feel comfortable with the action.

Now, right click on the folder and drag it to another part of the screen. If your operating system is Windows ME or Windows XP a menu appears giving you the choice of moving, copying or creating a shortcut to the new folder. Left click on Copy and another folder should appear on the screen.

Fig. 3.4 Menu after right clicking and dragging

Usually if you are asked to click a mouse and there is no indication of whether it is a right click or a left click you should assume that a left click is intended. This book will use that convention from here on.

Double clicking

Click twice, quickly, on your first new folder. This opens a window for the folder. There are no files in the folder. Close the window for the present by clicking the cross in the top right corner. Note that the clicks have to be fairly close together when you double click or it will not work. If after practising you still find difficulties with double clicking go to Chapter 10 which covers accessibility and where there are instructions on how to increase the time between clicks.

Windows desktop features

Taskbar

The main desktop feature of Windows is the **taskbar**. It allows you to switch between programs easily and lets you see at a glance which programs are open. It is the coloured bar which is normally found at the foot of the screen.

If you do not see it there it probably has the Auto-hide feature switched on. If you move the mouse to the foot of the screen it should appear. (If it doesn't come into view it may be along any of the other three edges of the screen.)

Your taskbar will look something like the diagram below but it will not necessarily be identical to it.

Fig. 3.5 The Windows taskbar

The button at the left of the taskbar is the **Start button**. If you click the Start button you will see the Start menu. To open a program, click the Start button and move the mouse up to **All Programs** (or Programs if you are using Windows Classic style). A list of programs then appears. Click on the program you want to open. The diagram below shows how to open the basic word processing program called WordPad. Click on Start, then point to Programs, then Accessories and finally click on WordPad.

After you have used a few programs Windows XP can list them above the All Programs button so that you don't even need to click this. Earlier versions of Windows such as Windows ME do not have this feature but all Windows programs back to Windows 95 have Start buttons which allow you to reach: **My Documents** where you can store files that you create or download; **Control Panel** where you can adjust your computer settings such as changing how fast your mouse works or altering the colours which Windows uses so that the screen is easier to read; **Search** which will help you find a file if you forget where you placed it; **Help**; **Turn Off Computer** or **Shut Down** to close your machine when you finish working.

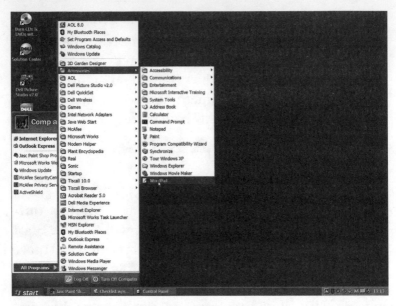

Fig. 3.6 Opening WordPad

To the right of the Start button you may see a row of icons (small pictures or symbols) like these:

Fig. 3.7 Quick launch icons for Outlook Express, Internet Explorer, and Show Desktop

This is the Quick Launch toolbar. If you click on any of these icons just once it will open the associated program. Clicking on Show Desktop removes whatever you are looking at onscreen and replaces it with the desktop view. Clicking the icon a second time returns you to whatever you had on screen to begin with.

Whenever you open a program, a 'button' for that program appears to the right of the Quick Launch toolbar. If you have more than one program open, these buttons offer a quick way to switch between programs. Just click on the button of the program which you want to see on screen.

Fig. 3.8 Taskbar with Paint Shop Pro and Works Word open

At the far right of the taskbar is a section known as the **tray** or **notification area**. Here you will find the clock and icons for programs such as antivirus software or your link to the Internet. Try hovering the mouse over each icon in turn to see what it represents. Hovering over the clock gives you today's date.

If you want to hide the clock or use the taskbar auto-hide feature, right click on the taskbar then click on Properties and adjust the checkboxes under the Taskbar tab (or General tab if using Windows ME).

Windows, Menus and toolbars

The blue band at the top of every window is called the **title bar**. It indicates the name of the program and the name of any file that is open. To move a window to a different position on the screen, click and drag the title bar.

Underneath the title bar in Works Word is a row of words that starts with **File** then **Edit** and finishes with **Help**. This is the **menu bar**. If you click on any of these words a **drop-down menu** appears that lists actions or **commands** that Word can perform. All Microsoft programs have menu bars which are very similar to this one.

Untitled Document - Microsoft Works Word Processor

| File | Edit | View | Insert | Format | Tools | Table | Help |

New...	Ctrl+N
Open...	Ctrl+O
Close	Ctrl+W
Save	Ctrl+S
Save As...	
Page Setup...	
Print Preview	
Print...	Ctrl+P
Send...	
1 C:\...\Checklist.wps	
2 C:\...\Chapter 3 Using your computer...	
3 C:\...\Chapter 2 Software Screenshot...	
Exit	

Fig. 3.9 Menu bar with drop-down menu

Below the menu bar at the top of the screen are one or
two rows of buttons each with a different icon. These
toolbars provide shortcut alternatives to some of the functions of the menu bar and again you will find that there are
many similarities across the Microsoft suite of programs.

Fig. 3.10 Toolbar buttons

At the far top right of the screen are three buttons which
are again common to all Microsoft programs. These are
the **Maximise**, **Minimise**, **Restore** and **Close** buttons
and they are known as the **control buttons**. There are
four options but you only ever see three buttons onscreen.
Maximise and Restore are opposite actions and share the
same button. (This is known as a **toggle** button.)

Fig. 3.11 Control buttons

If you move the mouse over to the top right of the screen and click on the **Maximise** button, the centre button, the window fills the screen so that you cannot see the desktop.

Clicking on the **Restore** button, also the centre button, returns the window to its original size.

If you click on **Minimise**, the first button, the window disappears from the screen but it can be reinstated by click-ing on its button in the taskbar. The Minimise button pro-vides another way of switching between screens when two or more programs are open.

Clicking the **Close** button closes the program completely and removes the button that was in the centre of the taskbar.

The **Restore** button also provides a way to switch between screens and can be useful if you want to see two different screens at the same time. If you move the mouse over the bottom right-hand corner of a window which has been re-stored (not maximised) the arrow head pointer changes from a single outline arrow to a double-headed line arrow. You can now click on the corner of the window and drag the corner to a new position so that the depth and width of the window changes. The double-headed arrow also appears when you move the pointer onto the edge of the window so that you can then expand or reduce just the depth or the width.

When you click on the **Restore** button to reduce the size of a window, sometimes scroll bars appear when the document is too large to fit in the window. They are found to the right and at the foot of the window. If you click and drag them they allow you to see different areas of a document.

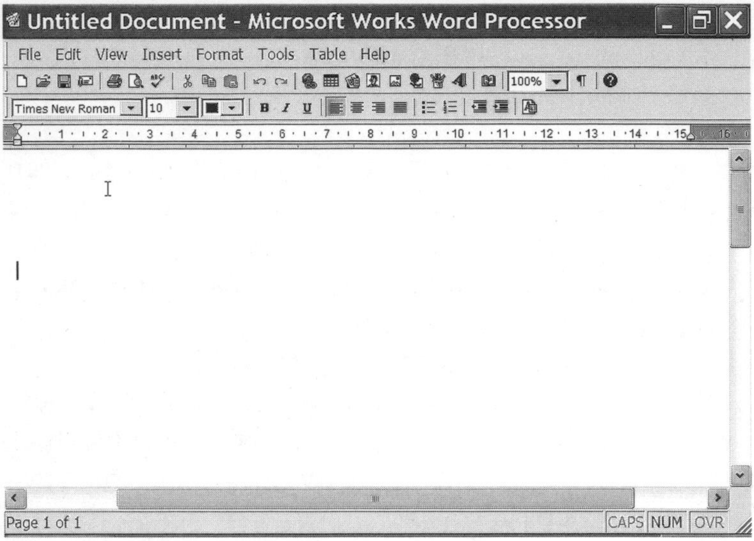

Fig. 3.12 Window with scroll bars

The square or rectangle that you click on within the scroll bar is called the scroll box. Its position provides an indication of which part of a document you are looking at. If you are near the end of a document the scroll box in the vertical scroll bar will be near the foot of the screen.

Fig. 3.13 Maximise button

If you click on the **Maximise** button so that the window fills the screen you will find that you can no longer change the size of the window by clicking and dragging the bottom right-hand corner.

Finally, note that you can also maximise, minimise, restore and close a window by clicking on the program icon in the title bar at the top left of the screen. The drop down menu which appears repeats the minimise, restore, maximise and close commands of the buttons at the top right of the screen.

Icons

Windows uses icons to represent programs, files, folders, shortcuts, hardware and system features.

As you learned in the section on the taskbar, a program icon will launch a program when clicked. However, if the icon is not on the taskbar, but is on the desktop or in a folder, then (for a standard set-up) you have to click twice (**double click**) to launch the program.

Internet Explorer

Outlook Express

Microsoft Works Word Pr

Jasc Paint Shop Pro 8

Windows Update

Acrobat Reader 5.0

Windows Media Player

Notepad

Fig. 3.14 Program icons

When you double click the icon for a document file, Windows opens the file with the appropriate program.

If you double click a folder icon it will open a window to display the contents of the folder which could be programs, document files or more folders.

Shortcut icons look like standard icons but have a curly arrow at the foot of the picture and often include the words 'Shortcut to...'. They allow you to create direct links from the desktop to files, folders or programs stored elsewhere in your computer.

Fig. 3.15 Shortcut icons

Some of the hardware that you will find represented by icons on your computer includes hard disk drives, floppy drives, DVD or CD drives, printers, scanners and cameras.

Hard Disk Drives

Local Disk (C:)

Devices with Removable Storage

DVD/CD-RW Drive (D:)

Fig. 3.16 Hardware icons

Windows also uses icons to represent certain key system features such as My Computer, My Documents and the Recycle Bin. My Computer is the first folder in your computer's filing system. All your files and programs can be reached from here. Double click its icon if it is on your desktop and you will see the hardware icons mentioned above. My Documents is the folder that Windows sets aside for the files which you create or download and the Recycle Bin is where you place files that you have finished with and no longer require.

My Documents   My Computer   My Network   Recycle Bin
                               Places

Fig. 3.17 System icons

Applications software such as Word and Excel also have icons. Here are the icons for Works Word and Works Spreadsheet.

Untitled   Works
Document   spreadsheet file

Fig 3.18 Works Word icon and Works spreadsheet icon

More on the Recycle Bin

When you drag a file that is stored on your hard disk to the Recycle Bin, or right click and select delete, the file is not really being deleted – it is being moved to a folder. You can rescue items from the Recycle Bin by right clicking and choosing Restore. This returns the file to wherever it was before it was moved to the Recycle Bin. However, note that when you delete a file on a floppy disk it does not go to the Recycle Bin and cannot be retrieved later.

If you want to free some disk space or 'permanently' delete the files there, right click on the Recycle Bin icon and click on Empty Recycle Bin. A dialog box will ask if you are sure and you then have to click Yes or No.

Files and folders

If you use a word processing program to write a letter, you can save the letter as a file in a folder on the computer's hard disk. After you have written a few letters you might want to organise them into different folders so that they are easier to refer to.

To create a folder, double click the My Documents shortcut on your desktop to open your My Documents folder. If you don't have My Documents on your desktop, you can locate My Documents by clicking on Start. The folder should either be in the Start menu itself or there will be a submenu under Documents that includes My Documents. Click on the menu entry to open the My Documents window on the desktop.

The next step is to click on the File menu, point to New and choose Folder. A folder called New Folder appears. Decide on an appropriate name for your folder and name it by typing over the reversed out lettering. By creating folders within folders you can build up a filing system that will enable you to find your files when you need them.

Fig. 3.19 Folder with subfolders

Remember, you can also create a folder by right clicking on the desktop, or in another folder, then pointing to New and clicking on Folder.

To rename a folder, right click on it then on Rename and overtype the name. You can also rename by clicking on the folder name once, pausing then clicking again to select the text so that it can be changed.

Folder windows

Does your My Documents window show large icons or small icons in the listing of folders and files when it is open on the desktop? To change your view of the window, click on the View menu (or Views button). You can then select from large icons or small icons or a list which includes details of file sizes and when files were created.

At the foot of the window is the **status bar** which indicates how many objects (files and folders) the window holds and the amount of disk space that they take up measured in bytes, kilobytes or megabytes. It also sometimes shows the amount of free disk space that there is available. If you cannot see the status bar, click View and select Status Bar

Earlier when learning about the mouse you created folders on the desktop then moved them by clicking and dragging. You can also click and drag files within and between windows but if you are using small icons or lists then it can be easy to make a mistake and to move something into the wrong folder. If you think this has happened you can undo the move by clicking on the Undo button on the window toolbar. If you do not see an Undo button on your toolbar you can add one by clicking on View, pointing to Toolbars then clicking on Customise. You can then choose the options that you want to see in your window toolbar.

Fig. 3.20 Undo button

A safer way to move a folder (or a file) is to cut and paste or copy and paste instead. To cut and paste a file onto the desktop, right click on the file then left click on Cut from the menu which appears. Next, right click on the desktop and left click on Paste from the menu. The folder then appears on the desktop.

You can also use Copy instead of Cut in the same way. This has the advantage that you still have a copy of the file in its original location if something should go wrong when you paste.

Once you have a hierarchy of folders in place you can reach your files by double-clicking down through your folders. If you want to work your way back up through the hierarchy you can click on the Up button on the window toolbar which looks like this.

Fig. 3.21 Up button

Clicking on the Folders button displays a second list of folders in a pane at the left of the window. This is **Windows Explorer** and it shows the hierarchy of all the folders on your computer. It allows you to move up and down through your folders and you can cut and paste or click and drag files or folders from the right-hand pane to another folder at any point of the hierarchy on the left-hand side.

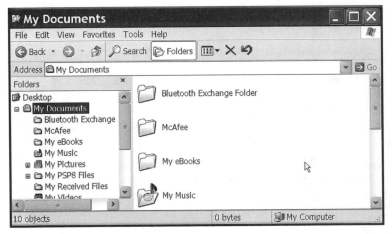

Fig. 3.22 Explorer bar

The folders in the left-hand pane are connected by dashed lines and some of them have pluses or minuses where the lines cross. A plus sign indicates that there are hidden subfolders. Try clicking on one to reveal them. The plus sign then changes to a minus sign. Click on the minus sign to hide the folders and return to the original view. If there are no plus or minus signs then it means there are no subfolders.

If you want to open a folder that you can see in the left-hand pane, click on it once. The right-hand pane changes to show the contents of this folder and the icon of the folder in the left-hand pane changes to appear as an open folder.

You can open Explorer from any window by clicking View, pointing to Explorer Bar and clicking on Folders. Alternatively, just right-click the Start button and click Explore.

Finding files

It can be frustrating if you inadvertently move a file into the wrong folder so that you cannot find it or if you simply forget where you saved it in the first place. If this happens you can search for it as follows. Click on Start, point to Search and click on All Files and Folders. A screen like this appears.

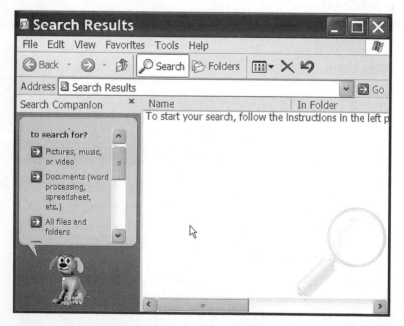

Fig. 3.23 Initial search window

Clicking on All Files and Folders gives this screen.

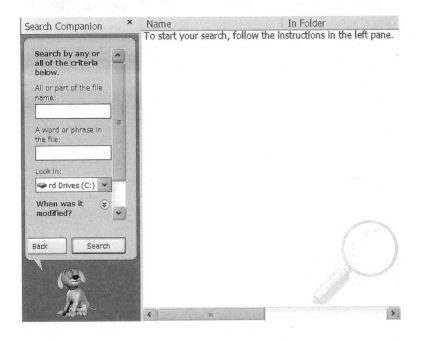

Fig. 3.24 Second search window

If you know the name of the file that you are looking for, enter it in the 'All or part of the file name' box. If you know roughly where a file might be you can narrow the search by selecting an option in the 'Look in' box. For example, if you know the file is definitely somewhere in My Documents then there is no point in searching the whole of the C: drive.

You can also narrow down your search by including words from the text in the 'A word or phrase in the file' box or you can search by date if you know when you last worked on the file.

Finally, click Search to run the search.

Move the mouse over any files which appear. The file name, file size, the date when it was last modified and the **path** to the file are displayed as a screen tip. The path looks something like C:\WINDOWS\INF which shows that in this example the file is in a folder called INF within the WINDOWS folder on the C: drive. You can double click the file icon in the search window to open it.

If you are not completely sure of the name of the file that you are searching for you can use **wildcard** characters in place of some of the letters or numbers. Use an asterisk to represent one or more letters or numbers or a question mark to represent just one letter. For example, Zo* will find all words that start with Zo but Zo? will find only three-letter words that start with Zo.

If you know the type of application that created the file you can include the filename extension. For example, a Word document would have a filename extension of 'doc' so a search for *.doc would bring up all Word files. Note that when including a file name extension it is crucial to include a dot between the main part of the name and the extension. For example, letter.doc specifies a Word document while money.xls indicates a spreadsheet; a web page would have a .htm extension and a help file would have .hlp.

Help

Microsoft includes a comprehensive database with Windows to help you find out more about the program and to assist you with any queries. Click on Start then on Help to open the Help resource.

The Help home page provides a list of topics that you

can browse through, an index, tours, tutorials, links to external help at Microsoft and a search engine. Try the search engine by keying Files into the Search box and clicking Go. The database is searched for all topics containing Files and these are then listed on the left of the screen. If you click on a topic such as 'Using files and folders' it displays information in the right-hand pane.

Open the index by clicking on the toolbar button. Type in the word that you want to find out about then select one of the topics which appears and click Display or double click the topic in the list.

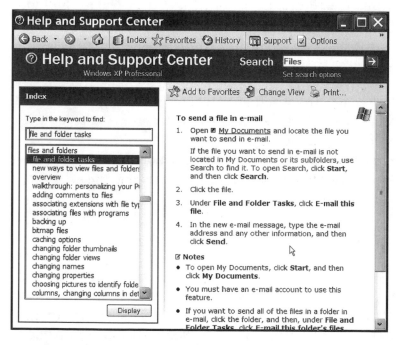

Fig. 3.25 Help screen accessed from the index.

In the next chapter which covers Microsoft Word you will

notice that Word like most Windows programs has its own Help system. It is, however, very much like Windows Help.

Formatting floppy disks

When a floppy disk is formatted its surface is divided into sectors which are then used to store your files. Most disks are pre-formatted but you can buy them unformatted in which case you will need to go through the following procedure.

Insert the disk to be formatted into the floppy drive then go to My Computer and right click on the floppy disk icon. A menu appears. Click on Format then choose Full format in the dialog box. Select the disk size under Capacity and click Start.

It takes about 2 minutes for Windows to format the disk after which the results are displayed telling you the size of each sector, whether there are any damaged areas that cannot be used and the total disk space available. Click Close to complete the process.

You can use the Quick format option if you want to simply delete all the files on a disk.

Customising

When you look at your screen you are looking at lots of tiny dots called **pixels** which together make up an image such as the desktop. The more dots there are, the sharper the image. A standard screen might have 800 pixels horizontally and 600 running vertically while a better screen might have 1400 x 1050 pixels. These numbers are known as the **screen resolution** and you can adjust your screen resolution to suit your monitor or your personal preference.

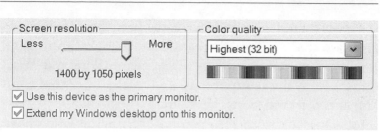

Fig. 3.26 Screen resolution and pixels

Click on Start then click on Control Panel. Double click Display to open it and click on the Settings tab. Click and drag the slider to change the resolution of your screen. Try different settings to see which suits you best.

After a while you might want a change of colour scheme or prefer larger type for title bars or icon names. Follow the instructions as if you were changing the screen resolution but this time click on the Appearance tab; or just right click on the desktop, choose Properties and then the Appearance tab. Experiment with different schemes. You can always change them back. If you want something really different, click on the Themes tab and choose More themes online. (You will need an Internet connection for this.)

Finally, click on Screen Saver and pick a screen saver program. Screen savers show moving images on your screen if you do not use the keyboard or mouse for a while. They were originally introduced to prevent screens from being damaged if left on but unused for a long time but nowadays they are more for fun.

Closing your computer

It is important not to just flick the on/off switch when you are finished working or otherwise you could damage your computer. First save and close any files then close every program that is open. Next click on the Start button and then on Shut Down. A dialog box appears asking you 'What do you want the computer to do?' Make sure that Shut Down is selected from the menu and click OK.

You can also restart your computer from the Shut Down dialog box. This option is useful if you install new software and have to restart your computer to complete the installation. Also, depending on your computer, you may also be able to put it into **hibernation** from the Shut Down dialog box. When hibernation is selected any document that is open is saved before the computer switches itself off. To restart the computer from hibernation, press the power button and any programs or documents that were open when you put the computer into hibernation will reopen onscreen.

To find out if your computer can hibernate, click Start, point to Settings then click Control Panel and double click Power Options. If your computer can hibernate there should be a Hibernate tab in the dialog box.

If your computer is switched on but you do not use it for a while it may automatically go into **standby** mode. In standby some of your hardware such as the monitor is switched off while the rest is put into a low power state. To start using the computer again, just press any key or move the mouse. Any documents or programs that were open when the computer went into standby will return to the screen.

Note that standby does not save your documents to disk so if you leave your computer for a while it is best to save your work first – or use hibernate if you have the option.

Occasionally you might find that everything on the screen

freezes and you cannot shut down the computer as described above. If this happens press the Ctrl key the Alt key and the Delete key all at the same time. Doing this once should produce a dialog box which allows you to close the programs which are open (and which may have caused the screen to freeze). Click End Task. This may free-up the screen. If it doesn't, press Ctrl, Alt and Delete again and the computer should shut down. If it doesn't you may have to resort to pressing the on/off switch on the computer case. When you do this you will find that the next time you start the computer it will run a program called Scandisk which will check your hard disk for any errors that might have arisen because of the improper shut down. Scan disk may take only a few minutes to run though it can take over an hour!

Maintenance

Scandisk (or Checkdisk)

It is a good idea to check you hard disk for errors every so often as errors may go unnoticed until it is too late and you can end up with damaged files.

There are two types of error that can afflict your hard drive – physical errors and logical errors. Physical errors arise from problems with the actual hardware. For example, if you drop your computer the read/write heads may 'crash' onto the disk surface and damage it. (See Chapter 2 for a description of how hard disks work.) Logical errors are more common and originate from problems with the way your files and folders are stored on the disk.

To prevent possible mishaps run Scandisk/Checkdisk as follows. Open My Computer then right click the icon for your hard drive (usually Local Disk C:) and click on Properties in the menu which appears. Click the Tools tab to reach the following screen.

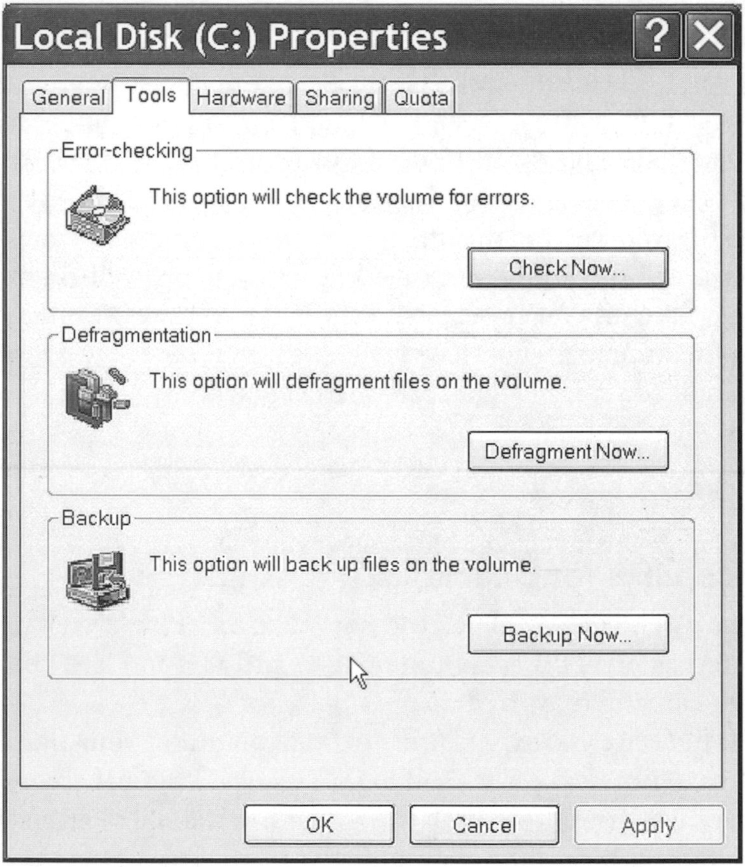

Fig. 3.27 Error checking and defrag screen

Click Check Now to open another dialog box. If 'Automatically fix file system errors' (XP) or 'Automatically fix errors' (ME) is selected then Scandisk will check for logical errors. In XP, if you also select 'Scan for and attempt recovery of bad sectors' Scandisk will check for physical errors. In ME, select 'Thorough' to check for physical errors.

Defragmenting

As you saw in chapter 2, all disks are divided into sectors. When a file is saved onto a hard disk it goes into one of these sectors. If there is not enough space in the sector to store the whole file the computer will place the left over data in other sector. If that one then becomes full it looks for more sectors until the file has been stored. This can result in file fragments being stored in different parts of the disk so the hard disk drive has to move between them when the file is next used. As you use files, amend them and resave them more and more fragments are created. Over time, this can slow down your computer. You can reorganise the data on your hard disk so that the fragments are all held close together by running a program called Disk Defragmenter.

To defragment your hard disk, open My Computer and right click the hard disk icon. Choose Properties then click on the Tools tab and click Defragment Now.

Windows Update

Windows Update is a free service provided by Microsoft to keep your version of Windows up-to-date. Microsoft regards it as an 'online extension of Windows that helps your computer work and run better'. Your computer may be automatically configured to check Windows Update for software patches to improve its security or performance but if you want to check that your system is up-to-date open Internet Explorer, click on Tools then choose Windows Update to be taken to Microsoft's Windows Update website.

Chapter 4
Microsoft Word - Part 1

Introduction

A word processing program like Microsoft Word allows you to write letters or prepare an application for a job without worrying about making mistakes. It enables you to key in your text, change it as many times as you want, check the spelling and grammar, change the size of type and the style of type, move sentences and change paragraphs around. You can save your work to complete it at another time then when you are satisfied that your document is ready you can print it. In addition, if you should spot a glaring error in your otherwise finished document you can quickly go back, make the change and reprint it.

Word is the leading Windows word processing program. It has a range of sophisticated features which allow collaborative working and even mathematical setting but it can also be used for simpler tasks or to learn about word processing. Although this chapter uses Word XP to demonstrate the features of a word processor, the examples given will also be relevant to users of Microsoft Works Word.

Starting Word

To start Word click once on the **Start button** to display the Start menu then move the mouse up to **All Programs** (or **Programs**). A list of programs then appears. Move the mouse onto this menu and click on **Microsoft Word** to launch the program. Alternatively, if you have a Word shortcut on your desktop, double click it.

Near the top of the screen is the **menu bar** (the row of words that starts with File, then Edit and finishes with Help). If you click on any of these words a **drop-down menu** appears that lists actions or **commands** that Word can perform. Each menu offers a range of commands but you don't need to know about all of them to use Word for straightforward tasks.

To open a new **document**, move the mouse pointer over the File menu and left click then move down the menu and click New. The screen should then look like this:

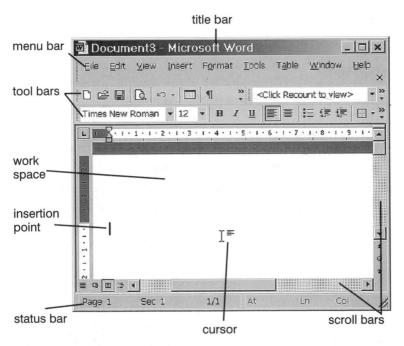

Fig. 4.1 A new Microsoft Word document

Possibly the most prominent feature of a new document is the flashing vertical line in the top left corner of the screen. This line is called the **insertion point** and it indicates the place on the page where the first letter or number will go when you press the key board. Sometimes you will also hear it referred to as the **cursor.**

As you key in text the insertion point moves to the right across the page as you type. If you click anywhere below text that you have typed, the insertion point moves to the end of the last word in your text.

Also, note that when the mouse is over the white work space it is shaped roughly like a capital letter 'I' but outside this area it reverts to its usual arrow head form.

Some useful keys

Pressing the **Backspace key** once deletes the letter to the left of the insertion point. The **Delete key** works in the same way but deletes text to the right of the insertion point.

Fig 4.2

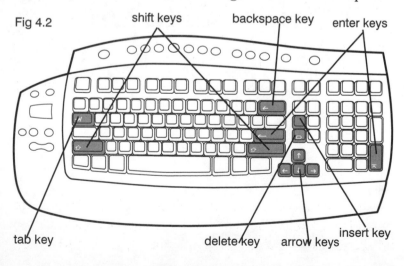

shift keys backspace key enter keys

tab key delete key arrow keys insert key

You can use the mouse to click alongside any word or letter that you want to change and use either the delete key or the backspace key to delete it. Alternatively, you can use the arrow keys to position the insertion point then make the deletion. The Up arrow moves the insertion point up one line, the left arrow moves the point one character to the left and similarly for the Down and Right arrows.

When you key new text in the middle of a sentence, Word inserts whatever you type at the insertion point and moves any text to the right of it along the page. This is known as Insert mode. Pressing the **Insert key** toggles (switches) Word into Overwrite mode where your typing overwrites what is on the page. Pressing Insert again, returns Word to Insert mode.

Word often automatically changes the first letter of the first word that you type into a capital letter, but to capitalise a letter manually you need to use the **Shift key**. The Shift key is found near the bottom left corner of the keyboard with a second Shift key near the bottom right corner of the main part of the keyboard.

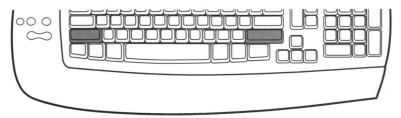

Fig. 4.3 Shift key location

Using the mouse, click just to the right of a letter that should be a capital but isn't. The insertion point moves from where you last typed to the point where you clicked. Press the Backspace key once then capitalise the letter you need by keying it at the same time as holding down the Shift key.

The Shift key is also used to type the symbols such as "!£%&*" that appear at the top of some keys such as the numbers near the top of the keyboard. Just press Shift at the same time as pressing a combined number/symbol key.

Pressing the **Enter key** moves the insertion point to a new line and is therefore used when starting a new paragraph or inserting a line of space between paragraphs.

When your typing fills a line Word automatically starts a new line. This is known as **word wrap**. If you were to press the Enter key at the end of every line as on a typewriter it would upset this word wrapping feature if you decided to go back and add or remove text. There are times, though, when you want to force the text onto a new line such as when you are typing an address.

When writing a letter you may also want to position your address at the right-hand side of the page. You can do this by using the Tab key. If you position the insertion point at the start of a line then press the Tab key the insertion point moves to the right and stops at a tab that has been preset by Word. If you continue to press the Tab key the insertion point moves to all the other preset tabs along the line. To position an address, type the first line then click at the start of the line and press tab until you find a position that suits.

Fig. 4.4 Tab key

Saving and naming a document

Word allows you to save and name documents so that you can keep them as a record on file or go back and amend them at a later date. It is good practice to name and save a document soon after creating it and then to save it from time to time as you work on it so that should your computer crash you will not lose work. Word does have a document recovery facility to help if your computer does crash but saving frequently is a good insurance policy.

To save a document that is open on your screen go to the File menu and click on Save As. A **dialog box** opens which asks you to choose a location to store your file and suggests a possible name for the file. To change the name to something more memorable just type on top of the blue highlighted name which Word has suggested.

Notice that when you save a document the title bar (the blue band at the very top of the window) displays the file name that you used.

Selecting text

Before you can move, or copy or change the style or size of text you first have to **select** it. To select a word click to the left of it and keep the mouse button pressed down. Next, move the mouse to the right so that the letters of your word appear white with a black background, then let go the mouse button.

This text has been selected.

Fig. 4.5 Selected text

You can also select a word by positioning the mouse over it and double clicking. If you want to select a whole paragraph, position the mouse over the paragraph and click three times.

To select a whole document, click on the Edit menu and then click on Select All.

To select several paragraphs of text, click at the start of your first paragraph then press the Shift key and keep it held down. Next, click at the end of the last paragraph that you want to work with and everything between the two click points becomes selected.

If you want to cancel a selection of text, click anywhere on the screen.

Copy, cut and paste

Being able to move text around within a document like this is one of the most useful aspects of word processing. You can move words, sentences and paragraphs within and between documents by using **Cut** and **Paste**.

To move a word, first select it then move the mouse up to the menu bar at the top of the screen and click on **Edit**. Move down the drop-down menu and click on **Cut**. Next click at the point in your text where you want the word to appear then move back up to the Edit menu and this time choose **Paste**. The word which you selected and cut is then placed in the new position.

When you click on Cut, the text which you selected is moved to a part of the computer's memory known as the **clipboard**. The main thing you need to remember about the clipboard is that it is temporary – anything placed here will disappear when you switch off your computer. You can see your clipboard by clicking **View** then **Task Pane** then **Clipboard**. The clipboard should then appear to the right of your screen. The clipboard can store up to twenty four separate items of text so you can reuse them as you work on a document. However, if you want to, you can work with Word without worrying about the clipboard as it will just do its job in the background.

An alternative to cutting and pasting is to **Copy and Paste**. The text goes through the same process as in cutting and pasting but this time the words that were selected remain in their original position as well as appearing in the position in which they are pasted. Select a word or sentence then click Edit then Copy. Click on the position in your text where you want the copied text to appear then choose Edit and Paste.

There are also keyboard shortcuts to copying, cutting and pasting. Having first selected your text, press the Control (Ctrl) key and X at the same time to Cut the selection and press the Control (Ctrl) key and C at the same time to Copy the selection. Pressing the Control (Ctrl) key and V at the same time pastes the selection from the clipboard into the document.

The Control key is usually found at the bottom left corner of the keyboard with a second Control key at the bottom right of the main part of the keyboard.

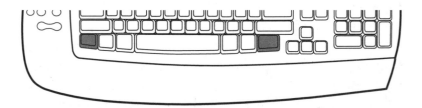

Fig. 4.6 The control keys

Toolbars

Below the menu bar at the top of the screen are one or two rows of buttons each with a different picture or **icon**. These **toolbars** provide shortcut alternatives to some of the functions of the menu bar. The toolbar which looks like this is called the **standard toolbar**.

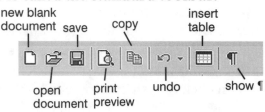

Fig. 4.7a Part of Word standard toolbar

Look for the following four icons on the standard toolbar: New Blank Document, Cut, Copy and Paste.

Clicking on the New Blank Document icon creates a new page. Note that the Cut and Copy buttons are 'greyed out' by default and will not work until you select some text.

The toolbar below the standard toolbar is called the **formatting toolbar** and looks like this.

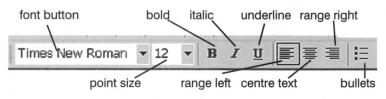

Fig. 4.7b Part of Word formatting toolbar

The buttons which you will probably use most are the Bold, Italic and Underline buttons.

Note that the Bold, Italic and Underline buttons are toggle

buttons (clicking once on a button applies formatting to a selected item and clicking a second time removes it).

Try selecting a word and clicking on the Bold button then select another word and try italic or underline. Next, select a word or phrase and click all three buttons one **after the other** to see how they can be used together.

If you make a change to a document but then decide that you would rather have left the text as it was previously, then you can undo your last change by clicking on the Undo button. It is usually found near the centre of the toolbar and looks like this.

Fig. 4.8 Undo button

Just to the right of the Undo button is the Redo button. It looks like the Undo button but has the arrow icon pointing to the right. The **Redo** button allows you to redo any action that you have just undone.

Another useful button is the **Show** button which looks lets you see all the spaces, paragraph returns and tabs in your document.

Fig. 4.9 Show button

The three formatting operations, bold, italic and underline, can also be applied using the keyboard rather than the toolbar. First select your text then press Ctrl + B for Bold, Ctrl + I for italic and Ctrl + U for underline.

Choosing a typeface

Words normal style of type or **font** is usually Times New Roman set at a size of 12 point and looks like this.

This is Times New Roman 12 point type.

The **Font** and **Font Size** 'buttons' on the formatting toolbar allow you to change the style and size of your type. If you click the arrow at the right of the Font 'button' a drop down menu of fonts or typefaces appears.

Fig. 4.10 Font and font size buttons

There are basically two families of fonts – called serif and sans serif respectively. Serif fonts have short straight or curved lines across the ends of the arms and stems of their letters. They are most easily seen when type is enlarged as in the following example.

Times is a serif font

Other popular serif fonts include: Century, Courier and Garamond.

'Sans serif' is taken from the French and means without serifs. Arial is a popular example of a sans serif font.

Arial is a sans serif font

San serif fonts are often easier to read on a computer screen which is why Arial is the default font for email programs such as Outlook Express while a font like Verdana is often used on web pages.

To change a font and typesize, select all the text in the document by clicking on the Edit menu and choosing **Select All** (or click Ctrl + A). Next, click on the arrow to the right of the Font button. A drop down menu appears offering a selection of alternative fonts or typefaces. If you choose Arial the type on your screen will change quite markedly. To change the size of your text again select all the text and choose a size from the drop down menu on the Font Size button.

Spelling and grammar

If you make a spelling mistake when typing, Word underlines the word with a wavy red line to bring it to your attention. You can either correct the mistake by retyping the word correctly or if you are not sure of the spelling you can right click on the word to see a list of options suggested by Word. If you know that you spelled the word correctly but it still has a wavy red line, right click on it and select the option to add the word to Word's dictionary.

Word brings grammatical errors to your attention by adding green wavy underlines to any text which it reckons could be presented better. This could simply be as a result of an additional space between words, a missing hyphen or a capital letter in the 'wrong' place. You can right click on the underlined text to see a suggested correction. If you want to find out more, choose Grammar or About this sentence when you right click.

Before printing a document it is worthwhile running it through Word's spelling and grammar check in case you missed any spelling mistakes earlier. You can do this by clicking on **Tools** then **Spelling and Grammar...** or by clicking the spell check button on the Standard toolbar which looks like this.

Fig 4.11 Spell check button

Printing

Finally, to print a document, click File then Print on the menu bar or click the **Print** button on the Standard toolbar.

Fig. 4.12 Printer button

If you click the Print button your document will be printed straight away but if you choose File then Print a dialog box appears which gives you some choices about what will be printed out. For example, you can choose to print multiple copies rather than just one, and in documents which extend to several pages you can choose to print just one page or a group of pages.

Recycle Bin

You can delete documents which you no longer want by moving them to the Recycle Bin. Go to the folder where the file is stored then either click and drag it to the Recycle Bin icon. Alternatively, right click on the file icon and choose delete. A dialog box opens to ask if you are sure you want to send the file to the recycle bin. Click 'Yes' to move the file to the bin.

Any file that you move to the Recycle Bin has not been permanently deleted. You can recover it by right clicking on the Recycle Bin icon and choosing **Open**. Next click on the file you want back then click **Restore** to return it to its original folder.

Closing and opening

To close a Word document you can either click **File** then **Close** on the Menu bar or click the Close Window button at the top right of the window.

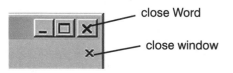

Fig. 4.13 Close window icon and close Word button from top right of screen

To close Word itself, click on the File menu then click

on Exit. Alternatively, click the **Close** button at the end of the title bar just above the Close Window button.

Finally, to open a Word document that you have previously saved and closed, click on the File menu then on Open. A dialog box appears on screen. Use the Look-in drop-down menu to select My Documents, or the folder where you stored the file, click on the filename and then on the Open button at the foot of the dialog box. The document should then open in its own window.

Summary Checklist

You now know enough to create, edit, save and print simple documents. Try writing a letter to a friend. You can use this checklist if you get stuck or click on the **Help** menu in Word and choose **Microsoft Word Help** to find out how you can get help while working in Word.

Start Word by clicking on the **Start button**. Move to All Programs then click on Microsoft Word. Alternatively, click the **Word button** on the Office toolbar.

Click on File then on New to create a new document or click the **New Blank Document button** on the Standard toolbar.

The **Backspace key** deletes text to the left of the insertion point.

The **Delete key** deletes text to the right of the insertion point.

Use the **Shift key** to capitalise a letter or to key the upper character in a combined key.

Use the **Enter key** when you want to force a new line.

Go to the File menu and click on **Save As t**o save a document or click the Save button.

Click **File** then **Close** on the Menu bar to close a document or click the Close Window icon near the top right of the screen.

Click **File** then **Open** to open a document or click the Open button on the Standard toolbar.

Click and drag to select text or double click to select a whole word or click three times to select a whole paragraph.

To copy/cut and paste, select the text then click the Copy/ **Cut** button. Click at the point in the text where you want to paste and click the **Paste button**.

Table of toolbar buttons covered in this chapter.

Click on **Tools** then **Spelling and Grammar** to use the spellchecker.

To print a document, click File then Print on the menu bar or click the **Print** button on the Standard toolbar.

To delete a file, drag it to the **Recycle bin** or right click on the filename and choose **Delete**.

Chapter 5
Microsoft Word – Part 2

This chapter builds on the topics covered in Chapter 4 – Microsoft Word Part 1 but please note that some of the features covered here are not available in Works Word.

Layout
Page setup

Your Word documents will most likely be printed on A4 paper in what is called portrait orientation which allows a line length which is not too long to read. If, however, you want to include a table or an illustration in your text then you may want to turn the paper on its side and use it in landscape orientation.

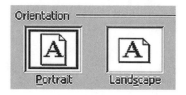

Fig. 5.1 Portrait and landscape orientation

To change the orientation of a whole document, click on the File menu and then Page Setup. On the dialog box which appears, click on the orientation that you want, check that Preview shows that it is to be applied to the whole document, then click OK.

If you want to change just one or two pages within a document you can do so by following this example. To change page 2 of a three-page document from portrait to landscape orientation, first click at the start of page 2, then click on File and Page Setup. Click 'Landscape' then go down to Preview, select 'Apply to this point forward' and click OK. All pages from this point forward are now landscape so go back to your document and click at the start of page 3 then click on File and Page Setup. Click 'Portrait' then go down to Preview, select 'Apply to this point forward' and click OK.

In the above example, Word separates the landscape page from the portrait page before it by placing it in a new section. Another new section is started when the layout reverts to portrait orientation. The section breaks between the sections are shown onscreen by a double dashed line across the page. Paragraph marks have to be switched on to see this.

Margins

Word surrounds your text by four margins: top, bottom, left and right; which together determine the overall width and depth of your text area. You can adjust these margins from the Page Setup menu to give you more room for your text, but be careful because if you allow your text to go too close to the edge of the page it may not print properly. If you click the default button at the foot of the dialog box any changes you make will become your default setting (i.e. will be used for all documents).

A4 paper has a long side of 29.7 cm and a short side of 21 cm. If you should ever want to use a different paper size you can adjust your page set up by clicking on the

Paper tab within Page Setup and choosing a paper size under from the drop-down menu.

Page numbers

Once you have decided the orientation of your document and the sizes of your margins, you might want to add page numbers that Word will update automatically for you if you amend or delete pages.

To add page numbers, go to the Insert menu and click on Page Numbers. A dialog box appears that allows you to choose whether you want the page number positioned at the bottom of the page in the footer area or at the top of the page as a header. The dialog box also gives you five options for aligning your page numbers: right, left, centre, inside and outside. The last two options allows you to position page numbers as books sometimes do where left-hand pages have the page number at the bottom left and right-hand pages have the page number at the bottom right (or the other way around).

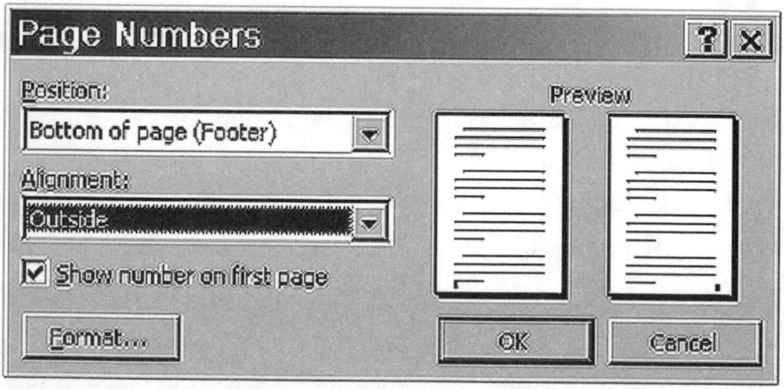

Fig. 5.2 Page with outside page numbers

Click on the Format button in the Insert Page Numbers dialog box to choose whether you want to number your pages with letters or Roman numerals as an alternative to the usual Arabic numbers.

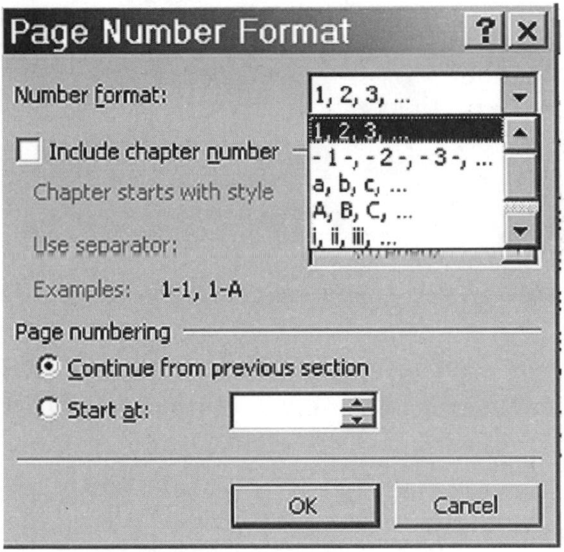

Fig. 5.3 Page numbering options

You can also insert page numbers using the Header and Footer toolbar which is covered next.

Headers and footers

A page header is a strip of space in the top margin of every page in a document into which you can insert text such as the title of the document, or perhaps a graphic such as a company logo. A footer is the equivalent space in the margin at the bottom of the page. If you click on File, then Page Setup then Layout you can see exactly how far your headers and footers are positioned from the top and bottom of the page.

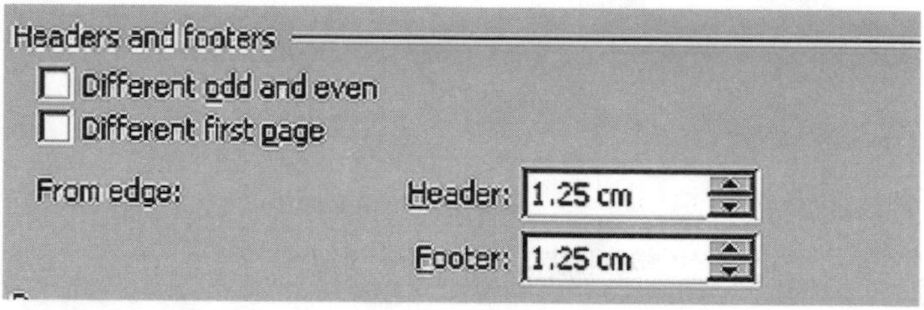

Fig. 5.4 header and footer distances from page edge

You might expect to use the Insert menu to add text to a header or footer but in fact you need to go to the View menu. If you click on View then Header and Footer the Header and Footer toolbar appears. The text in your document turns grey and cannot be worked on but the header and footer areas become 'active' ready for you to add some text.

Fig. 5.5 Header and footer toolbar

The main features of the toolbar that you might want to use immediately are explained in the following table.

Fig 5.6

Icon	What it does
	Inserts a page number
	Inserts the number of pages in the document
	Formats the page number - choose from numbers, letters or Roman numerals
	Inserts the date
	Inserts the time
	Page set up - choose whether you want different headers or footers on left and right pages or not to have a header or footer on your first page
	Switches between the header and footer

If you click on Insert and point to AutoText a drop-down menu appears with a choice of possible header or footer entries such as 'Created on' or 'Last printed'. In both these cases Word automatically inserts the relevant date. If you choose 'Page X of Y', Word again inserts the appropriate page numbers.

Word has three preset tab options to make it straightforward for you to place your header/footer text at the left of the page, in the centre or to the right.

Formatting

Word 1 covered some of the basic formatting options such as choosing alternative fonts and applying bold, italic and underline from the formatting toolbar. This section looks again at these options as well as some others that are available from the Format menu.

Format – Font

By clicking on Format then Font you can see all the options that you have for choice of typeface (Abadi to Westminster), typesize (8 point to 72 point) and font style (regular, bold, italic and bold italic).

These options can all be accessed from the toolbar but the Format menu also gives you a choice of effects such as:

Shadow, Outline and Emboss

In addition, if you click on Format, then Font, then Character Spacing you can then add space between the letters of your chosen typeface to expand it or reduce the space to condense it.

Normal... expanded... condensed

You can even add animations such as Marching Ants or Las Vegas Lights by clicking on the Text Effects tab – but these can only be viewed properly on screen.

If you don't want to create your own styles but want a design that has more impact than normal text then click on Format then Themes to see a library of style themes that you can use instead.

Format – Paragraph

Click on Format then Paragraph and select the Indents and Spacing tab to change text alignment, text indentation and line spacing.

Under the General section of the Indents and Spacing tab you can choose to left align, right align, centre or justify your text. Text which is centred sets the middle of each line of text in the middle of the page. In text which has been left aligned, the first word of each line is exactly the same distance in from the left edge of the page – like this paragraph. In right-aligned text the last word of each line finishes the same distance in from the right of the page, while text which has been justified is both left aligned and right aligned. All four of these formatting commands can also be applied from the Formatting toolbar using the following icons (which appropriately illustrate the above explanations).

Fig. 5.7 Left aligned, right aligned, centred and justified buttons

Indentation moves text in from either the left (or right) margin. This can be useful if you want to bring attention to a section of text such as a list or a quotation. To indent a paragraph, first select it then click on Format then Paragraph and select whatever indent you require under Indentation. For example, this paragraph has been left indented by 1 cm. Note that you can even select an indent with negative value (an outdent) which moves text into the margin area.

The indentation section of the Format – Paragraph dialog box also has a Special option which you can use to set an indent for the first line only of a paragraph or a hanging indent where all the lines of a paragraph are indented except the first line – as in this paragraph. The Formatting toolbar again offers a shortcut to setting indents – although you have to accept the indent values which have been preset. Look for the following icons to increase or decrease an indent respectively.

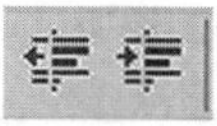

Fig. 5.8 Increase and decrease indent icons.

The spacing between lines of text is usually single-line spacing but you can increase it to 1.5 lines or to double-line spacing for effect or to make text easier to read. If you select 'Multiple' you can choose any line spacing you want in half line increments from 0.5 line spacing to 50+ line spacing and beyond! Just enter the number of lines you require in the At box.

Format – Bullets and numbering

Lists can be used to make text easier to read or give it more impact. For example, it can be more helpful if the ingredients for a recipe are presented in a bulleted list rather than in a continuous paragraph. In the same way, a numbered list can help when presenting the instructions for the recipe where the order of the instructions is important.

Bullets

To create a bulleted list, first position the insertion point where you want the list to appear. Next click on Format then Bullets and Numbering and select the Bullets tab to see the range of bullet styles that Word offers. Select a style that you like and click OK. The first bullet then appears in your document. Type the first entry in your list and press Enter. The second bullet then appears on the next line where you can type the next entry, and so on. When you get to the end of your list and press Enter to start a new line, a bullet will appear. To remove it, press the Backspace key twice to stay on the same line, or press Enter again to leave a line space between your list and the next paragraph.

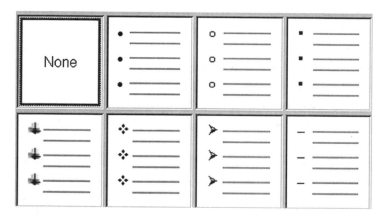

Fig. 5.9 Bullet styles in Word

If you decide that you don't like the style of bullets you have chosen for your list you can change it, or remove the bullets altogether, by going back into Format, Bullets and Numbering and selecting another style or None on the Bullets tab.

You can also apply bullets by clicking the Bullets button on the formatting toolbar instead of going into the Format menu. The bullets button will apply the style of bullet which you selected on your last visit to the Format menu.

Fig. 5.10 Bullets icon

Numbered lists

To build a numbered list, again position the insertion point where the list is to be set then click Format, Bullets and Numbering and select a style from the Numbered tab. Key in your list pressing Enter after each entry. If you want to include a line in the list that doesn't get numbered, press Shift and Enter (instead of Enter) at the end of the line before which the unnumbered line is to appear. The Shift + Enter key combination is shown by the ⏎ symbol. This is also known as a **soft return**.

As with bullets, you can create a numbered list by clicking the Numbering button on the formatting toolbar instead of going into the Format menu. The Numbering button will apply the style of numbering which you last selected.

To include several levels of numbering within one list go to Format, Bullets and Numbering and click on Outline Numbered tab and choose a style and start creating your list. The list below uses numbers, letters and Roman numerals to indicate three levels. To go down a level, press Tab after you press Enter at the end of a line. To go up a level, press Shift and Tab.

1) Follow these instructions when creating a multilevel list.
   a) Press enter and tab to go down a level.
   b) Press Enter to stay on a level.
      i) Press enter and tab to go down a further level.
      ii) Press Enter to stay on a level.
   c) Press Enter then Shift and Tab to go up a level.

2) Press Enter then Shift and Tab to go up a level
      i) Press Enter then Tab twice to go down two levels in one move

Borders and shading

Word's Borders and Shading commands give you the opportunity to add straightforward decoration to a document which can add impact to a notice or poster.

To add a border to a paragraph or group of paragraphs, first select the text then click on Format then Borders and Shading. On the Borders tab choose whether you want a box, shadow or 3D border to be set then select a line style, colour and width from the menu alongside. You can check what your border is going to look like in the Preview and decide whether you want the border to apply to all edges. For example, if you think it might look better with just a horizontal line at the top and bottom of your selection, click on the icons which show side borders to switch them off.

To apply a border to a whole page, click the Page Border tab. It is very similar to the Borders tab but gives you the option of applying the border throughout the document or to certain pages only.

Other useful features of the Format menu

You can present your text in two or three columns and adjust the sizes of each column. Click on Format then Columns to see the options available.

Click on the Change Case option in the Format menu to change selected text to sentence case (new sentences start with a capital), lower case, UPPER CASE, Title Case or tOGGLE cASE (switches upper case to lower case and the other way round). Toggle case can be particularly useful if you accidentally hit the Caps Lock key rather than the Shift key.

Background allows you to add a colour background to your page with different fill effects such as textures, patterns and gradients (shading).

Use AutoFormat if you want Word to automatically apply heading styles and list styles or to replace certain text features – for example, straight quotes can be replaced with smart quotes or fractions replaced with fraction symbols. After your document has been autoformatted you can choose a design by clicking on Format then Themes.

Insert menu

The Insert menu is handy if you want to include additional features in your document such as:

Page breaks or section breaks

Page numbers

Symbols (^{TM},©,®,†,ç,≤ etc.)

Images or clipart.

Page breaks are useful when you want to force text onto another page. If one part of your document finishes half way down the page and you want to start a new section on a fresh page, you could press the Enter key as often as it requires until a new page appears. However, you may find it easier simply to click on Insert, then on Break and select Page break. If you click on the Show button you will see the page break as a broken line across the page at the point where you inserted it.

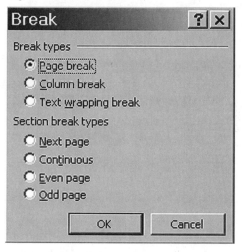

Fig. 5.11 Insert page break dialogue box

Section breaks are useful when you want to change the text that appears in headers or footers such as when you change chapter in a book. To change a header but keep page numbers running continuously, choose a Next page section break. The main text becomes greyed out but the header and footer areas can be amended. Make sure that 'Same as previous' does not appear above the first header/footer of the new section or the previous section's header/footer text will appear instead. You can toggle 'Same as previous by clicking on this button on the headers and footers toolbar.

Fig. 5.12 Same as previous button.

To insert page numbers choose Insert then Page numbers. You have a choice of where to place the number on the page and if you click on the Format button you can select a style of numbering to suit.

Symbols can be very handy features if you want to emphasise or clarify text with arrows, mathematical symbols, Arabic characters or pictorial icons. There is a wide range of choice from desert islands 🏝 to telephones ☎. Click Insert then Symbol and select Webdings or Symbol from the Font menu in the window which appears.

If you require bigger pictures to illustrate your document then take a look at the clip art files which are supplied with Word. You may have to choose to include media files when you first install Word but you can also download clipart from Microsoft's Web site. To add an item of clipart, click on Insert then point to Picture and click on Clip Art. The Task Pane opens at the right of your screen. Just type in a description of the item you are after and click Search. You will then be presented with a choice of many possible images. For example, searching on 'computer' produced the following:

If you have image files that you want to place in a document, again use the Insert Picture option but this time select From File. A window then appears from which you can browse for the file that you want to insert.

Tables

If you ever have to present lists of information such as names and addresses then the Tables feature of Word can be a great help. It is so useful it even has its own listing on the menu bar!

A table consists of rows and columns of cells into which you can place text or graphics. You can use tables to create a framework that holds text in place. For example, you could use tabs to lay out this Christmas list but it might be easier to use a table and to hide the borders.

Name	Gift
Jean	Scarf
Richard	CD
Lesley	Book

To add a table to a document, click Table then Insert table. A dialog box appears which allows you to choose the number of rows and columns that you need for your table. Don't worry if you select fewer rows or columns than you need, you can always add more later.

If you choose the default setting of five columns and three rows with Auto selected under 'AutoFit behaviour - Fixed column width' then a table is opened which extends across the width of your page. You can choose different fixed column widths by scrolling through the list.

If you know that you are not going to want a table that extends across the whole page, choose the option to AutoFit to contents. A table like this appears:

You can also insert a table by clicking on the Insert Table icon on the standard toolbar and selecting the rows and columns that you need as shown below.

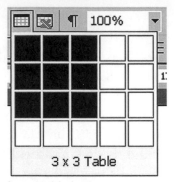

Fig. 5.13 Using the Insert table button

To insert text into a table just click on a cell and start typing. As you insert your text the columns expand to the required width.

If you want to start a new line within a cell, position the insertion point before the word that you want to start the new line and press enter.

You can further adjust the width of the columns or depth of the rows in your table by moving the mouse onto an edge then clicking and dragging to the required position.

You can use the arrow keys to move between the cells of the table, or you can use the tab key. (If you want to actually tab text within a table cell, click Control and the tab key together.) Pressing the tab key moves the insertion point from cell to cell towards the right. Pressing Shift and the tab key together moves the insertion point to the left. If you press the tab key when the insertion point is positioned in the last (bottom right) cell of the table, a new row is added to the table.

You can also add rows from the Table menu as follows. Click on a row of the table that is either above or below where you want the new row to be added. Go to the Table menu and click Insert then choose the 'Row above' or 'Row below' option as required.

To delete a row, first select it by clicking just to the left of the table. Next click Table then Delete rows.

You can add (and delete) columns in the same way, just substitute 'column' for row in the above procedures.

If you want to select just one cell in a table, move the mouse to the edge of the cell so that a solid black arrow appears then click. You can then copy or cut the contents of the cell as required.

To move an entire table, position the mouse over the top left corner of the table so that the Move handle appears then click and drag the table to its new position.

You can show or hide the borders to individual cells or an entire table by selecting the cells then choosing which borders you want to see from the Borders button on the toolbar.

Fig. 5.14 Borders button

This column of figures is actually a table with most of its borders hidden. The table was selected and all the borders removed then the bottom right cell was selected and top and bottom borders added for that cell.

	£50.79
	£34.88
	£105.30
Total	£190.97

The total in the bottom row was even calculated using the table menu. (The formula =SUM(ABOVE) was used after clicking on Table then Formula.)

The standard table style is called Table grid but if you want something more stylish you can select from a range of options by clicking the AutoFormat button on the Table menu. The table below uses the Contemporary style.

Fig 5.15a

Contemporary	Style
	Table entry
	Table entry

You can access the AutoFormat option when you first create your table by clicking the AutoFormat button in the Insert Table dialog box.

The contemporary style table above might look better if the words 'Contemporary' and 'Style' appeared in the same cell. One way that you can achieve this is by merging cells as follows. Select the cells to be merged then click Table then Merge cells.

Fig 5.15b

Contemporary Style	
	Table entry
	Table entry

Different views

Word provides a range of ways in which you can display your document onscreen. The topics which follow can, with one exception, all be accessed from the View menu.

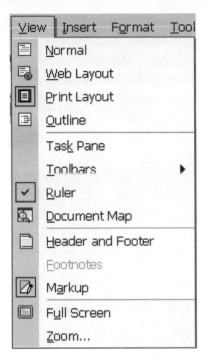

Fig. 5.16 Drop down View menu

Normal view shows your text on a white background with no edges or borders and when you move on to a second page the page break is a dotted line across the page. When scrolling through a long document it is the fastest view to use but it does not necessarily show everything on the page. For example, headers and footers (see below) are not displayed. To select Normal view, either click on the View menu and then on Normal or go to the bottom left corner of your page at the left of the scroll bar just above the status bar and click the Normal view button.

In Print layout view you can see how text and graphics will appear when printed. To see print layout view click on the View menu and choose Print Layout. The screen changes so that you can see the position of your text relative to the top, bottom and side margins. It also shows separate pages for each page of your document. If you prefer to work in this view but find that scrolling between pages is time consuming you can hide white space at the top and bottom of the page by clicking on the dark band that separates the pages.

Web Layout view is intended for those who want to create web pages using Word. It can still be useful even if you are not writing web pages because the text wraps to fit the Window size reducing the need to use scroll bars. Web Page Preview shows you what your Word document will look like if saved as a Web page and viewed in Internet Explorer.

Outline view shows the structure of your document and indents headings and text according to their level in the document .

If you click on View then Task Pane a frame opens to the right of your page. If your task pane is set to New Document you will see a list of documents that you worked on recently and options for opening a new blank document or a new document from template. To display a list of other task pane options, click on the downward pointing arrowhead at the top right of the task pane. If you click on Clipboard you will see items that you copied or cut onto the clipboard since you last opened Word. If there is nothing on the clipboard, select some text and click the Copy icon on the Standard toolbar. You can use this view of the clipboard if there is an item of text that you want to use several times within a document. While you have the task pane onscreen, open a previously saved document and change to Web Page view to see the benefit of not having to use the horizontal toolbar.

Click on View then Document Map if you are working on a long document and want to check where you are within it. A new pane then opens on the left and displays the chapter and section headings within the document. Note, however, that the document must have had heading styles applied for this to work (see section on headings).

Sometimes you need more room on your screen to see as much as possible of your text. To hide all the tool bars, title bar, etc. click on View then Full Screen. Your page then fills the screen and a small toolbar appears to enable you to close the full screen view when you need to see you toolbars again.

If you want to increase or reduce the size of your text onscreen, click on View then Zoom. A dialog box appears from which you can choose set magnifications of 75%, 200% or page width by clicking on the option buttons but if you scroll the Percent box you can pick any magnification from 10% to 500% in steps of 1%.

If you look at the any Word drop-down menu you will see that some of the entries have a small icon as well as a text entry. These icons match the icons that are used in Word's toolbars so if you see an icon in a menu entry it may also appear in a toolbar.

To see the full extent of Word's toolbar options, click on View then Toolbars. Those toolbars with a tick alongside their entry in the list are already on your screen. This drop-down list is not even the full list of options. Click on Customise to see the full list.

Try adding another toolbar such as Tables and Borders.

Click View, Toolbars then Tables and Borders. The toolbar appears on screen within your work area. Click on the title area of the toolbar so that crossed double-headed arrows appear then drag the tool bar to the foot of your screen. It should drop into place underneath the scroll bar and above the status bar.

At the right-hand end of every toolbar is a small downward pointing arrowhead. If you hover over it with the mouse it displays the screen tip Toolbar options. Click on Toolbar Options then move the mouse onto Add or Remove buttons then Tables and Borders (you don't need to click). A menu of buttons appears. Click on one of the options that is not already ticked to add another button to the toolbar.

At the left-hand end of every toolbar is an icon consisting of a column of short horizontal lines. This icon acts like a handle for the toolbar. Click on the Tables and Borders handle and drag it left or right to reposition the toolbar then drag it onto the work space area. To remove the toolbar from the screen, click the close button at the top right or go back to the View, Toolbars menu and deselect it there.

Fig. 5.17 Toolbar handle icon

One toolbar which is not included in the View, Toolbars menu is the Header and Footer toolbar which has its own entry in the View menu. This toolbar lets you insert text such as chapter titles or page numbers in the top (header) and bottom (footer) margins of the page.

Click on View then Header and Footer – the Header

and Footer toolbar appears and the page view instantly changes to Print Layout view, if you were not already working in this view.

Print preview

Print Preview is an option you might want to consider just before you click on the print button to send your document to the printer. Print Preview gives you a better idea of what your printed document will look like and it will probably save you a lot of paper over time! Click File then Print Preview or look for the Print Preview icon on the Standard toolbar. If everything spaced as you would like you can click on the Print icon in Print Preview or if you want to make amendments, click Close to return to your original screen.

Fig. 5.18 Print preview icon

Mail merge

If you want to send the same letter to a number of different people you can make the task a lot easier by using mail merge.

To set up a mail merge you need the text of the letter that everyone will receive and a separate table of names and addresses of all the recipients. Don't worry if you do not have a table of names and addresses to start with – Word's mail merge wizard will help you create one as you go along.

To start the wizard, click on Tools then point to Letters and Mailings and click on Mail Merge Wizard. There are six steps to the wizard:

Step 1

Choose the type of document that you want to create – click on Letters.

Step 2

Select the document that you want to start from. If you have already typed your letter, choose Start from existing document, otherwise choose Use the current document.

Step 3

This is where you select your recipients from an existing list or table or type a new list – choose 'Type a new list' then click on Create. A window called New Address List appears.

Fill in the address details for the first person then click New Entry an d fill in the details for the next and so on. When you have completed your list, click on close and give your database of names and addresses an appropriate name.

Step 4

Now write your letter but don't put in any addresses and don't put in any greeting line. Instead click on the Address block link in the wizard and choose the way in which you want the address to appear. Repeat this step for the Greeting line.

Step 5

Now preview your letter.

Step 6

Finally, you can print your letters or make last minute

adjustments to particular letters should you want to make some more personalised.

And that's it – you will have performed your first mail merge and, hopefully, saved yourself a lot of time in the process.

Chapter 6
Microsoft Excel

Have you ever wished that you had a better idea of your monthly costs and expenditure? If so, then a spreadsheet program like Excel could be what you are looking for. Using Excel you can create different categories of expenditure such as groceries, car, clothing or entertainment. You then key in the cost of everything you buy during the month and get Excel to add it all. If you want to, you can display the results as a chart so that you can get a better picture of how much you are spending in each area.

◇	A	B	C
1			
2			
3	Date	Description	Cost
4	1-Jun	Rent	£ 400.00
5	1-Jun	Electricity	£ 20.00
6	15-Jun	Gas	£ 20.00
7	30-Jun	Transport	£ 150.00
8	30-Jun	Entertainment	£ 100.00
9	10-Jun	Credit card	£ 400.00
10	7-Jun	other	£ 50.00
11			£ 1,140.00
12			
13			
14			

Fig. 6.1 A spreadsheet program like Excel can help you track your household budget

Getting started with Excel

Open Excel by clicking on Start then Programs and choosing Excel. Alternatively, use a short cut icon if you have one on a toolbar. Excel opens and you see a **workbook** on screen. A workbook is Excel's name for a file. Each workbook consists of three or more **worksheets** which you can switch between by clicking the tabs called Sheet 1, Sheet 2, etc. at the foot of the window.

An Excel window has a lot in common with a Word window. At the top of the screen are the Excel menus which contain familiar entries such as File, Edit, View, etc. together with a new one – Data. Below that you probably have the Standard and Formatting toolbars visible with a Task pane off to the right of the screen. Check these toolbars are toggled on by clicking on View then Toolbars.

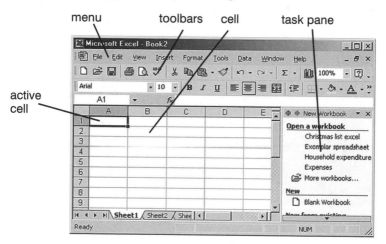

Fig. 6.2 Excel worksheet

Each worksheet is a grid of boxes called **cells** into which you can place descriptive text, or numbers or a formula that performs a calculation. Click anywhere on a worksheet. The cell which you clicked on now has a bold border around it. This is the equivalent of the insertion point in Word. If you key a number it will go into this cell which is known as the **active cell**.

Each row of cells in a worksheet is identified by a number and each column of cells is allocated a letter. This enables every cell in the worksheet to have a unique **cell reference** made up of a column letter and a row number. For example the first cell in a worksheet has cell reference A1.

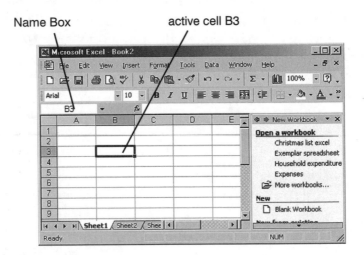

Fig. 6.3 Cell references plus Name Box

Each worksheet has more cells than you will probably ever use. After the first 26 columns a second letter is introduced so that the next 26 columns are labelled AA, AB, AC through to AZ then the next 26 columns become BA, BB, BC through to BZ. The final column is actually IV which makes 256 columns in total. There are even more rows – 65,536 to be precise. If you have time to spare you can check this by scrolling down through all the rows but it is a lot easier to click on the **Name Box** which appears just above the A column heading and key in a cell reference such as IV65536 and press Enter. This will move the active cell to the very last cell on the worksheet.

You can find the cell reference of your active cell by checking the Name Box but if you also look at the top of the column above the active cell you will see that the box with the letter in it is a blue colour, while if you look to the left of the row which contains the active cell you will find that the row number is also blue.

Entering a number

To enter a number into a cell, just click the cell to make it active then key in the number. The number appears at the left side of the active cell. If you check the status bar at the foot of the worksheet window the word Enter should be visible. To complete the procedure and **enter** the number you can either: press the Enter key, press the Tab key or just click on another cell.

If you press the Enter key, the number moves across to the right of the cell and the cell below becomes the active cell.

Pressing the Tab key instead of the Enter key also moves the number across to the right of the cell but the cell in the next column to the right becomes the active cell rather than the cell below.

If you click on any other key, Excel completes the entering procedure for you and the cell that you clicked on becomes the active cell.

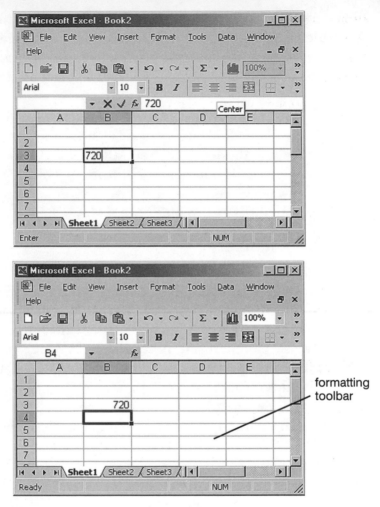

Fig. 6.4 a & b Entering a number into Excel

Entering text

To enter text, click a cell to make it active then key in the word and press Enter or Tab. Note that the word remains on the left of the cell. Excel left-aligns text and right-aligns numbers by default. You can change this if you wish by selecting a cell then clicking on the Align Left, Center, Align Right or Justify buttons on the For-matting toolbar.

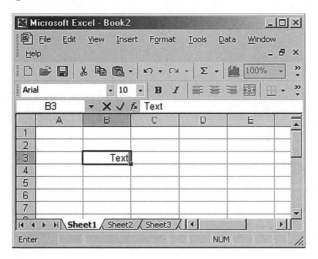

Fig. 6.5 Entering text into Excel

Selecting a range of cells

To select several adjacent cells, click on the corner of a cell then drag the mouse to highlight the required cells. If the cells that you want to select are not side by side, just press Control and click each cell that you require.

To select an entire row or column of cells, move the mouse over the row number or column letter. A solid black arrow appears. Clicking once will highlight the row or column.

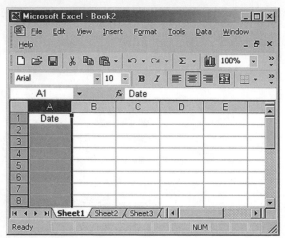

Fig. 6.6 Selecting a column

Changing column widths

If you enter a longish word such as 'Spreadsheet' into a cell then the word may extend beyond the area of the cell. If you enter text or a number into the cell to the right, Excel hides any overlapping text from the cell with the long word.

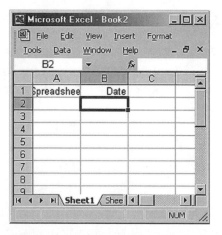

Fig. 6.7a Changing column widths with AutoFit

You can widen the column with the long word by first clicking on the column heading to select the whole column.

Next go to the Format menu and choose Column then click on AutoFit selection. The column width adjusts to fit the length of the word. You can also adjust the width of a column manually by clicking on the column border next to the column heading and dragging to the required width.

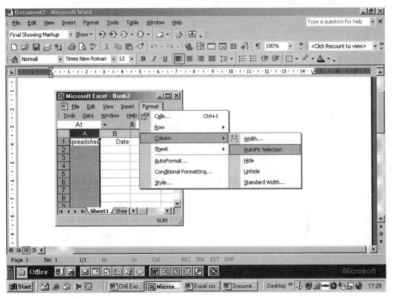

Fig. 6.7b Changing column widths with AutoFit

Editing a worksheet

To edit the contents of a cell just click on the cell and key in the new entry or amend the existing entry by clicking and selecting the parts to be changed as you would do in Word. You can also edit entries in the **Formula Bar** which appears just above Column C and extends across the screen so there is more room if you are editing a long title.

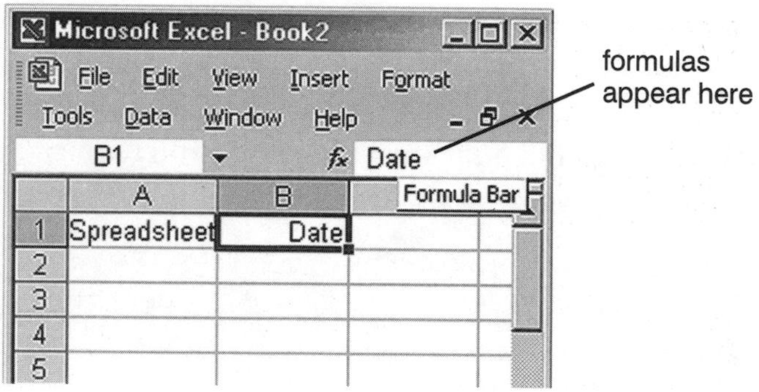

Fig. 6.8 Formula Bar

A quick way to remove the contents of a cell is to right click on the cell and choose **Clear Contents**. This removes the contents of the cell but leaves the cell in position. There is also a Delete option when you right click on a cell but be careful if you use this option as it deletes both the contents of the cell and the cell itself which means that another cell is moved to take its place. This can upset your spreadsheet.

Number formatting

When formatting text in Word you can change the font, size, style and alignment. You can also do this in Excel but you can also select a **number format** for the figures which you place in the cells of your spreadsheet. To select a number format, click on Format then Cells and select the Number tab. The menu which appears offers a range of options. There are five which you will find helpful at this point.

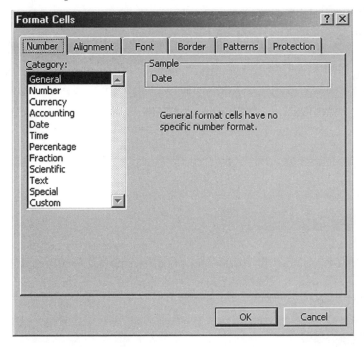

Fig. 6.9 Format /Cells/Number tab

General format is Excel's default format but it has several peculiarities. For example, when you enter a number such as 105.00 into a cell what actually appears in the cell is 105 – the 'trailing zeros' do not appear. You may therefore prefer to use the **Number** format if you want to specify the number of decimal places and the **Currency** or **Accounting** options when working with money. The accounting format differs from the currency format in that it aligns decimal points and currency symbols when working with a column of figures.

To convert a cell to currency format, select the cell then click Format then Cells and on the Number tab choose Currency. Make sure that the £ symbol is selected in the menu that appears in the right of the window and click OK.

The fifth number format that you might find useful is the **Date** format. If you key a date into a cell, Excel often recognises that it is a date and applies this format. However if you go to the Format cells, Number tab you can select how you want dates to be presented, for example: 01/01/05 or 1 Jan 2005. Make sure that 'English (United Kingdom)' is selected under Locale.

AutoFill

AutoFill is a feature of Excel which helps when either copying entries or when you want to increment entries (increase them step-by-step). It will work with both numbers and dates. To use AutoFill to create a column of dates, enter the first date into a cell and apply a format as described above. Next, click on the cell and position the mouse over the bottom right-hand corner of the cell so that a bold cross appears (the fill handle). Now, click and drag down the column until you reach the last row that you are likely to need. Excel fills the column with consecutive dates. You can amend this column of dates by clicking on the AutoFill options icon. A dropdown menu appears offering a range of options. For example, you can choose just to display week days or for consecutive months or years to be shown instead of days. You can also copy the date in the first cell into all the other cells in the column and you can choose to apply just the formatting without any data in the cells.

You can use AutoFill with the other number formats that are mentioned above to copy cells, fill a series of entries or apply a format.

Adding with Excel formulas

Adding in Excel is just like ordinary arithmetic except the program does the laborious bit for you. For example, to add the contents of two cells, you enter the cell references (e.g. A1, A2) in a third cell along with a + sign and an = sign, press Enter and that is it! So if cell A1 contains 105 and cell A2 contains 20 we could add the amounts by placing the **formula**

=A1+A2

in another cell, say A3.

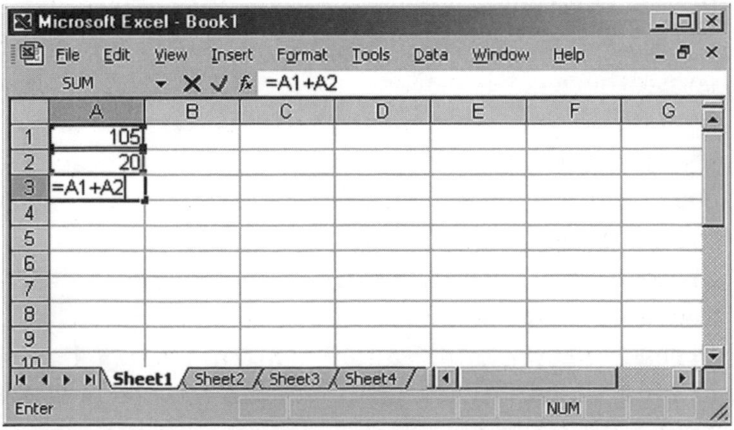

Fig. 6.10 Two cells being added. Show formula in third cell

121

Note that a formula always begins with an equals sign (=). If this order looks a little unusual think of it as saying that the contents of cell A3 equals the contents of A1 added to the contents of A2.

Try this addition on your spreadsheet. Open a new worksheet then key 105 into cell A1 and press Enter. Next key 20 into cell A2 and press Enter. Now put the formula =A1+A2 into cell A3. You don't need to add any space between the parts of the formula. Excel displays the cell references in the formula in different colours and uses the same colours to highlight the actual cells. Press Enter to carry out the calculation and see the answer displayed in cell A3.

Arguments and operators

In the formula =A1+A2 the cell references are known as **arguments** while the addition sign is known as an **operator**. Other operators that Excel allows are – (subtraction), * (multiplication) and / (division).

Try subtraction, multiplication and division on your spreadsheet.

Click on the fill handle of cell A1 and drag it across to copy the number 105 into cells B1, C1 and D1. Do the same for row 2.

In cell B3, key in the formula to subtract cells B1 and B2 (=B1-B2) and press Enter.

In cell C3, key in the formula to multiply cells C1 and C2 (=C1*C2) and press Enter.

In cell D3, key in the formula to subtract cells D1 and D2 (=D1/D2) and press Enter.

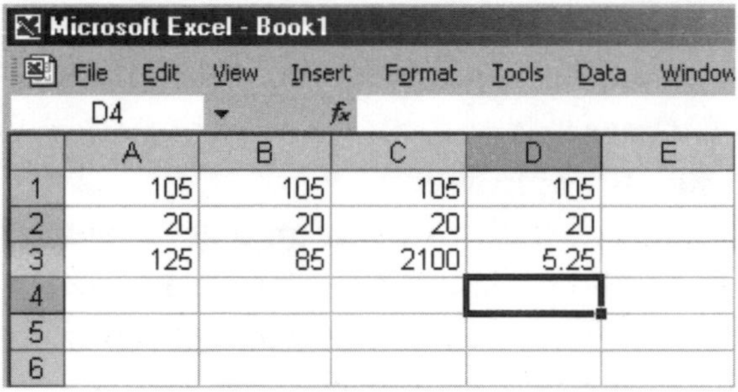

Fig. 6.11 Answers to previous exercise

More arguments!

Your calculations in Excel are not limited to just two arguments. For example, to add a list of numbers you could extend the formula to include many more cell references, e.g. $=A1+A2+A3+A4+A5$.

You can also combine operators – such as in the formula to calculate an average. In this case the formula is $=(A1+A2)/2$. Note that you need to add brackets to indicate to Excel that A1 and A2 need to be added before the division by 2 takes place. Otherwise, Excel will add half the value of A2 to A1.

SUM function

There is an easier way to add a list of numbers than the method outlined above and that is to use Excel's SUM function. A function is just a formula that has been already set up by the designers of Excel. To use the SUM function to add up a list of numbers, all you need to do is enter the cell references for the first and last cells. For example, to add a list of five numbers which appear in cells A1, A2, A3, A4 and A5 you type:

=SUM(A1:A5)

in the cell where you want the answer to appear, (say cell A6) and then press Enter.

The numbers which you add up do not have to be arranged vertically. You can add up along a row as well. Try using the SUM function. Enter numbers into cells A1 to A4 on your spreadsheet then type

=SUM(A1:D1)

in cell E1 and press Enter.

Note how Excel first highlights cell A1 in colour then the colour border extends to cover all the cells in the calculation. You can click and drag this coloured border if you want to change the cells that are included in the calculation.

AutoSum

An even faster method is to use the AutoSum function. Click on the cell where you want the total of the calculation to appear then click on the AutoSum button on the Standard toolbar.

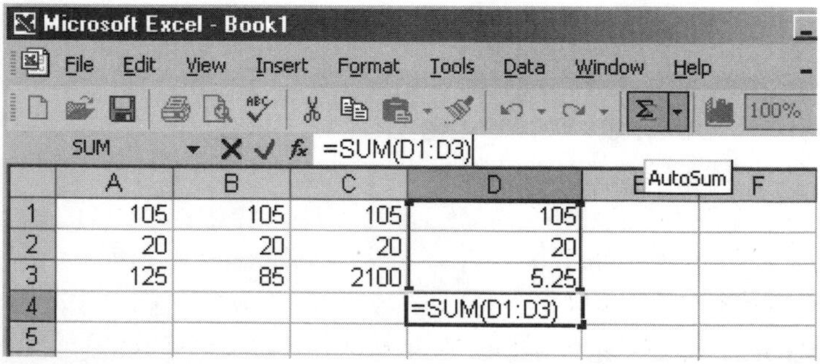

Fig. 6.12 AutoSum button

When you click the AutoSum button Excel fills in the function details for you and even suggests the range of cells to be added. Click Enter if the range is the one you wanted or amend the cell entries to the correct ones. You can do this by keying in the correct cell references or by clicking and dragging the flashing colour border until it is in the correct position.

Cutting, copying and pasting

You can cut, copy and paste cell contents just as you would do in Word. First, make your selection by clicking on the cell that you want to cut or copy then click Edit followed by Cut or Copy. A flashing line appears round the selection. This is known as a **marquee**. Next select the cell where you want to place the contents of the original cell and choose Edit followed by Paste.

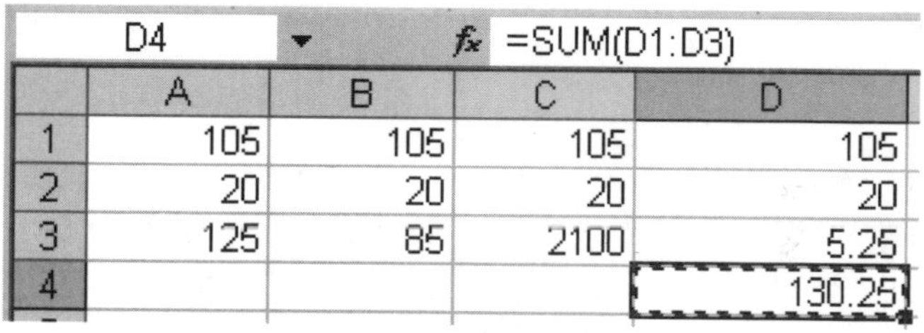

D4	▼	*fx* =SUM(D1:D3)	
	A	B	C	D
1	105	105	105	105
2	20	20	20	20
3	125	85	2100	5.25
4				130.25

Fig. 6.13 Marquee

You can also use the toolbar buttons to Cut, Copy and Paste or you can click and drag from one cell to another. To move a cell's contents by clicking and dragging, click on the cell then move the mouse pointer onto the bold border of the cell. When the mouse pointer changes to a crossed arrow, click and drag the cell contents to its new location. If you want to copy the cell contents, hold down the Ctrl key when you click and drag.

If the cell that you want to move or copy contains a formula you might find mistakes appearing in your spreadsheet. Here is an example that should help explain why.

On a new worksheet, type 4 into cell A1 then press Enter.
Next, type 3 into cell A2 and press Enter.
In cell A3 type the formula to add cells A1 and A2 (=A1+A2) and press Enter.
The figure 7 appears in cell A3.

Move to column C and type 5 into C1 and press Enter.
Type 5 into C2 and press Enter.
Now click on cell A3 and copy it then move to cell C3 and click Paste. Cell C3 should display the number 10 and if you click on it the formula =C1+C2 appears in the formula bar.

Excel automatically changed the cell reference from A3 to C3 in the formula when you transferred it from column A to column C. A cell reference which can be changed in this way is called a **relative cell reference**.

Go back to column A in your spreadsheet and type 0.175 into cell A4.
Now click on cell A5 and type in the formula =A3*A4 then press Enter.

Excel multiplies the contents of cell A3 by 0.175 which is the same calculation you would do if calculating the VAT on an item (multiplying by 0.175 being equivalent to multiplying by 17.5 and dividing by 100).

Now copy cell A5 and paste it into cell C5. This number 0 appears in C5. The calculation has not worked because the cell references were relative (i.e. could be changed by Excel) and cell C4 is empty.

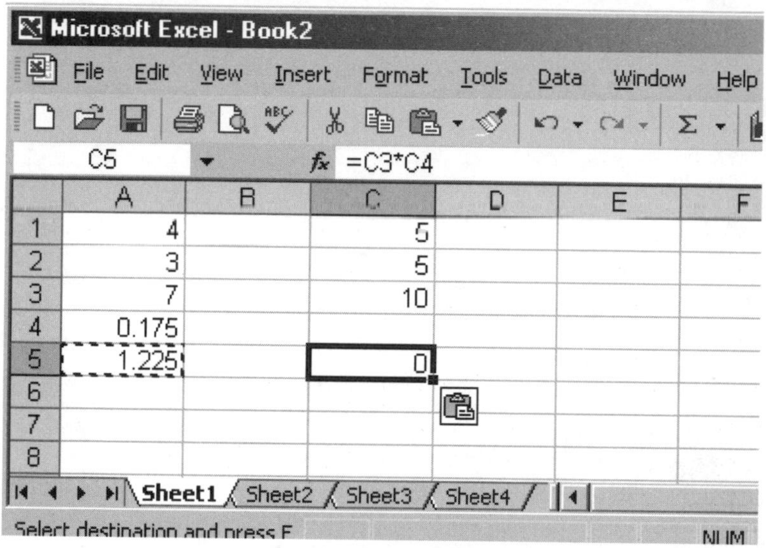

Fig. 6.14 Relative cell reference producing wrong result

Instead of using relative cell references, we need to use **absolute cell references** which do not change when they are copied between cells. An absolute cell reference is created by adding a dollar sign in front of each column and row reference. For example, click on cell A5 then go to the formula bar and insert dollar signs so that the formula looks like this:

=A3*A4

Now copy cell A5 and paste it into C5. This time the

calculation works because Excel does not change the absolute address A4.

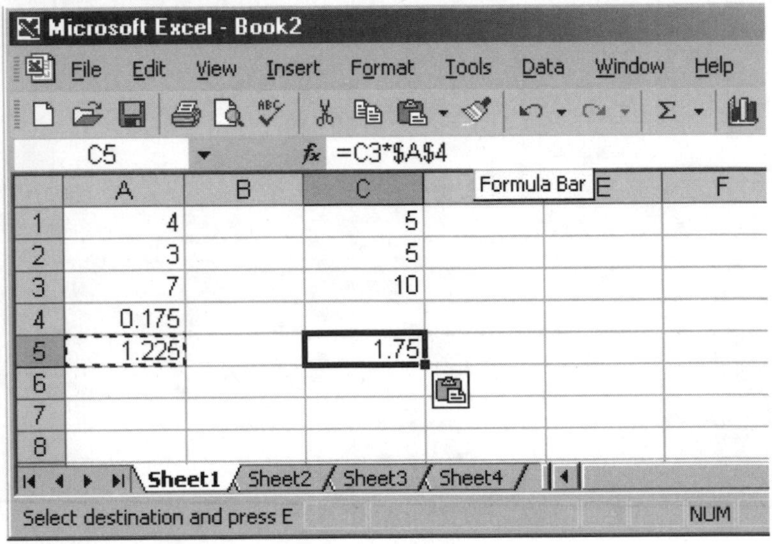

Fig. 6.15 Using absolute cell references

Inserting rows and columns

You will often need to insert new rows or columns as you build a spreadsheet. To insert a new row above an existing row, click on the row heading to highlight the row then go to the Insert menu and click on Insert then on Rows. To insert a column to the left of an existing column, click on the column heading to highlight the column then go to the Insert menu and click on Insert then on Columns.

Build a budget spreadsheet

Try creating a simple spreadsheet to track a household budget like the one below:

	A	B	C	D	E	F	G	H	
	E23	▾	fx						
	A	B	C	D	E	F	G	H	
1	Monthly Spend								
2	Day	Payee	Total	Food	Car	Fuel	House	Other	
3	2	Electricity	£19.00				£19.00		
4	2	Insurance	£16.07				£16.07		
5	2	Garage	£82.85		£82.85				
6	4	Supermarket	£26.42	£26.42					
7	7	Gas	£30.00				£30.00		
8	7	DIY store	£16.43				£16.43		
9	8	Garage	£91.97		£91.97				
10	9	Supermarket	£9.91	£9.91					
11	12	Phone	£30.00				£30.00		
12	14	Supermarket	£66.52	£40.46		£26.06			
13	16	Mortgage	£420.00				£420.00		
14	16	Postage	£10.50					£10.50	
15	16	Night out	£37.96					£37.96	
16	19	Supermarket	£26.69	£26.69					
17	23	Supermarket	£25.43	£25.43					
18	25	Petrol station	£20.49			£20.49			
19	27	Supermarket	£24.08	£24.08					
20	28	Council tax	£150.00				£150.00		
21		TOTAL	£1,104.22	£152.89	£174.82	£46.55	£681.50	£48.46	
22									

I◄ ◄ ► ►I / Costs \ **Dec 03** / Oct 03 / Sept 03 / August 03 / July / I◄ |

Ready | | | | | | | NUM | |

Fig. 6.16 Household expenditure spreadsheet

First decide on the different categories that you want to keep track of and use these for your column headings. This spreadsheet SUMs each column. For example the total for the Food column is calculated using the function =SUM(D4:D21), while the car column is =SUM(E4:E21), and so on. The spreadsheet also adds up the total for every row because, for example, petrol was bought at the supermarket on the 14th. However, you don't have to key in different details for each row. Just key in the first one – put =SUM(D4:H4) in cell C4 and press Enter. Next click on C4 to make it the active cell and click and drag the cell border down the column until it covers all the rows that you want a row total for and release the mouse button. Excel automatically inserts the correct cell addresses within the brackets of the SUM function.

If you have not already inserted formulas for the column

totals, you can repeat the above procedure along the Total row. In the example shown you would click on cell C22, key in =SUM(C4:C21) and press Enter then click and drag along the row to cell H22.

You can change the alignment of your columns, add border rules, change fonts or add colour by selecting the cells that you want to emphasise then clicking Format and choosing Cells. This brings up the Format Cell dialog box that was used earlier to select categories for numbers. Applying some of the features available under the Alignment, Font, Border and Patterns tabs can make your spreadsheet more readable.

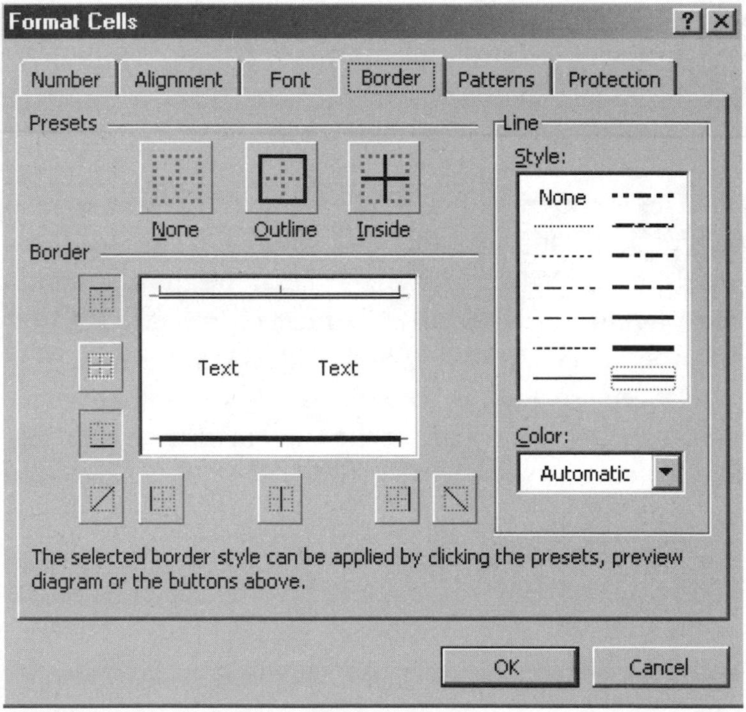

Fig. 6.17 Format cells dialog box

Excel charts

You can make your spreadsheet even easier to read by converting it into a chart using Excel's Chart Wizard.

Step 1

Click on the Chart Wizard button on the Standard toolbar and in the first window which appears choose the pie chart option and click Next.

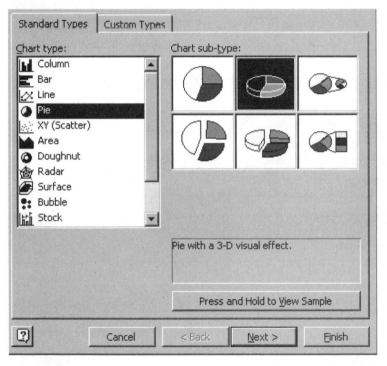

Fig. 6.18 Step 1

Step 2

In this step you have to select the data that you want to appear in the chart. Minimise the dialog box by clicking on the icon to the right of Data Range. Now hold down the Ctrl key and select the column heading cells: Food, Car, Fuel, House, Other. Keeping the Ctrl key held down, select the cells which show the totals for Food, Car, Fuel, House, Other. The two cell ranges appear in the Data Range box. Select the Data in Rows option and click Next to complete Step 2.

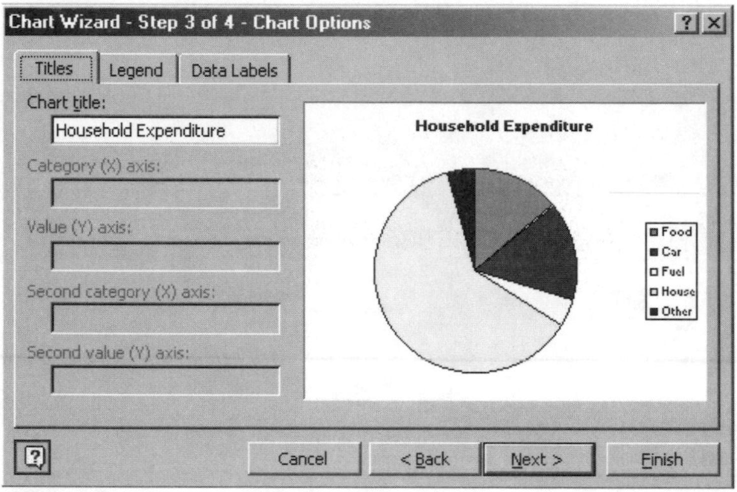

Fig. 6.19 Step 2

Step 3

Give your chart a title and then click Next.

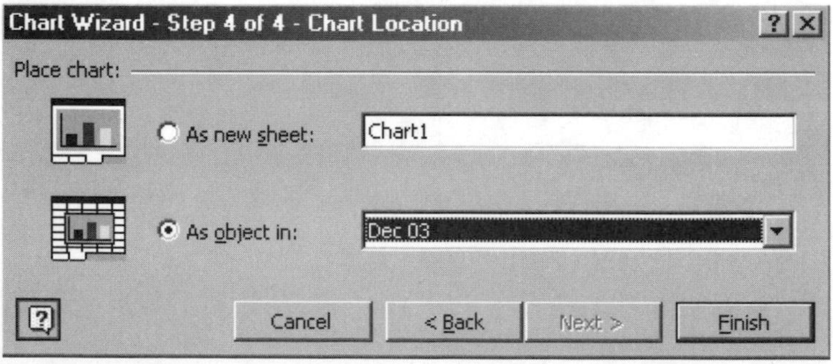

Fig. 6.20 Step 3

Step 4

Finally, decide whether you want the pie chart to appear on the same worksheet as your data or in a separate worksheet.

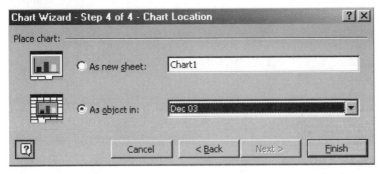

Fig. 6.21 Step 4

Your pie chart should look something like the one below.

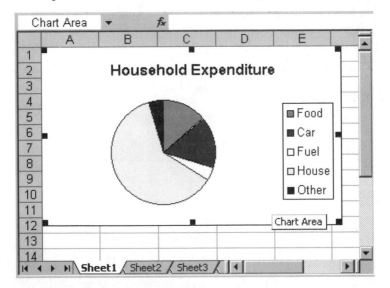

Fig. 6.22 Household expenditure pie chart

This gives you a graphic representation of monthly spending but it might be a bit more useful with more information on it. Move the mouse over the white space next to the pie chart then right click and choose Chart Options.

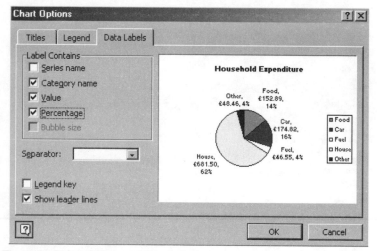

Fig. 6.23 Chart Options – Data Labels

This opens the dialog box that you used in Step 3 above. This time, click on the labels tab and select Category Name, Value and Percentage. These labels then appear in your diagram as shown below.

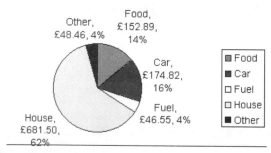

Fig. 6.24 Pie chart with labels

This chapter has introduced the main features of Excel. There is a lot more that you can learn about the program but hopefully you can now use it productively to handle everyday costs and calculations.

Chapter 7
Microsoft Internet Explorer

What is the Internet?

The Internet is a worldwide network of networks containing millions of computers all linked by phone lines, optical cables and satellite links. The computers which host the Internet are owned and run by universities, government bodies and businesses. The computers in these organisations follow a common set of rules or **protocols** so that their computers (and your computer) can communicate with one another.

To connect to the Internet from home, you need a computer with appropriate software and a modem, a phone line and an **Internet Service Provider (ISP)** – an organisation such as a telephone company or cable TV supplier through which you access the Internet.

How is the Internet used?

Most people use the Internet for electronic mail (email) or to access web sites on the World Wide Web (WWW) but other features of the Internet include newsgroups, Web logs or 'blogs' and instant messaging.

The World Wide Web

The World Wide Web is like a vast electronic library which you can use to find information or entertainment. It is also a marketplace where businesses and consumers can buy or sell goods and services. So what advantages does the Web have to offer over traditional ways of working? Here are some examples.

- Online shopping offers either more convenience or more competitive prices. You can buy your weekly shopping online from supermarkets such as Tesco and Sainsbury and have it delivered to your door (although usually there is a delivery charge). Alternatively, if you are buying a holiday or arranging a flight you will find that it can be much cheaper to purchase from the Web than from a high street outlet.

- Many banks now offer online banking which has the advantage that you can have access to your account at any time of the day. You can see your current balance, pay bills, set up direct debits or apply for a loan all from your home. Online accounts often also offer better rates of interest than traditional accounts.

- For over two hundred years the Encyclopedia Britannica was one of the world's best known reference sources. It used to cost around £1000 for a full set but today you can access it and other reference publications such as dictionaries and thesauruses online, for free or a fraction of the cost of a printed book.

- Traditionally printed newspapers also now have online competition. Newspapers can have perhaps two or three editions per day at best but online news organisations can update their pages as news breaks giving an almost instantaneous reporting of important events from all round the world.

If you want to view a Web site, you key the Web site address into a program known as a **browser**. Microsoft's browser is Internet Explorer but there are others such as Netscape Navigator. Your computer then makes a phone call to a computer at your Internet service provider. This computer then looks for the computer that has the Web site that you were looking for and links your machine to it. Computers which provide information on the Web like this are known as **Web servers**.

It is estimated that the Web contains hundreds of millions of pages of information. Many of these pages have **hyperlinks** which enable users to navigate between Web pages and Web sites by clicking on words or images. This **'surfing'** is possible because most Web pages are written to an internationally agreed format called **HTML** (Hypertext Markup Language) which can be displayed in any browser.

A Web site address consists of the 'www.' prefix, a domain name which is usually the name of an organisation and an extension such as '.co.uk'. For example, entering www.bbc.co.uk into Internet Explorer and pressing the Enter key will take you to the BBC's Web site.

Some domain name extensions are used globally, such as .com, while others are country-based, such as .co.uk.

.com usually signifies a business – often an American or a multinational company

.biz is also used by business

.co.uk is used by British companies or for the British versions of an international site

.gov is used by government sites

.org usually indicates a non-profit organisation

.net is used by network providers
.edu is usually an American educational site
.ac.uk is used by British universities

The idea that there are hundreds of millions of pages on the Web can be quite daunting but there are two main ways in which you can find the information or Website that you are looking for. You can use a **search engine** such as Google or a **directory** such as that provided by Yahoo! With a search engine you type in a key word for the topic you want and the search engine then displays a list of Web sites that cover your subject.

Fig. 7.1 Google UK home page (Reproduced with permission)

Directories are more structured. With a directory you

choose a category such as 'sport', then a subcategory such as 'golf' and so on until you are presented with a selection of likely Web sites.

Fig. 7.2 Yahoo! directory. (Reproduced wth permision of Yahoo! Inc. YAHOO! and the YAHOO! logo are trademarks of Yahoo! Inc)

Email

Email is one of the most popular aspects of the Internet. It allows you to communicate easily with friends or family all over the globe. You could send a message to someone on the other side of the world when it is 3.00 p.m. locally and the message will arrive in their mail box at their ISP almost instantly, ready for them to download in the morning – you don't have to contact them directly like a phone call. You can also send the same email to several people just by including their email addresses in the message header.

Email messages need not only be limited to text. You can send graphics and photographs as attachments to your emails. (See the next chapter on Outlook Express.)

If you want to be able to check your email on any computer you should consider Web-based email such as that provided by Hotmail (www.hotmail.com) or Yahoo! (www.yahoo.com). You can then check your email wherever you are by logging on to the Internet.

Newsgroups

Newsgroups are online communities which communicate via electronic discussion boards that are part of the Usenet system. There are over 30,000 newsgroups. Think of a specialist topic and there is probably a newsgroup for it.

Messages which are posted to a newsgroup are placed on the message board and **threaded** so that readers can see the flow of the conversation and who has said what. Some newsgroups are moderated to filter out inappropriate postings but most are not moderated. In addition, users of newsgroups often use **screen names** to remain anonymous so language can be direct and arguments are not unknown.

Usenet is technically similar to email except that the messages are public. This is why an email program like

Outlook Express can be used as a **newsreader program** as well. When you access a newsgroup you go through your Internet service provider's news server which may only support a selection of the many newsgroups that are available.

If you are away from home and cannot access a newsgroup through your ISP you can still read and post messages over the Web through Google Groups which can be reached from the Google home page.

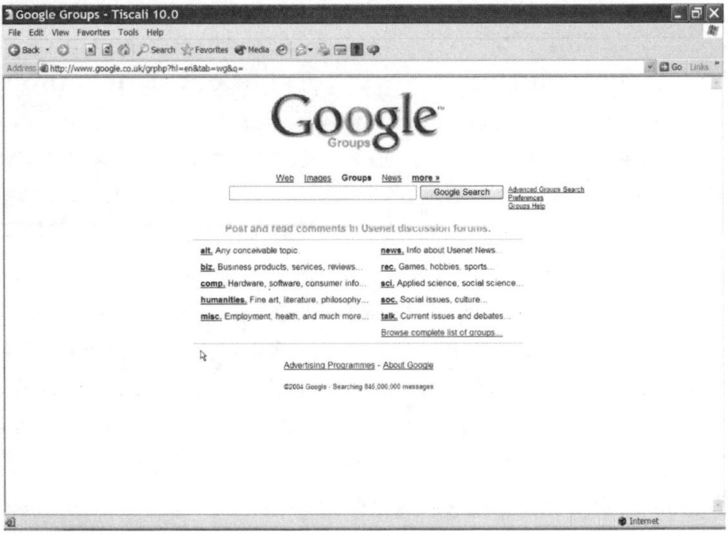

Fig. 7.3 Google groups

Newsgroups are communities with their own customs and idiosyncrasies so if you are new to newsgroups it is usually recommended that you read without posting for some time to learn how they operate. Reading without posting is known as **lurking** which sounds distasteful but there are usually more who participate by reading than by posting. Failure to adhere to the customs of a group has been known to lead to a **flame attack** (personal insults) on a 'newbie'.

Blogging

A Web log or **blog** is a Web page that is like an online diary or journal consisting of short snippets of information that are arranged chronologically with the most recent posting at the top of the page. A good blog will be updated frequently and include Web links and commentary about its core topic.

Like a diary a personal blog might list personal activities, opinions about books, music, films and websites the only difference is that it is online – but you can choose whether or not share it with the rest of the world. Other blogs take a wider view and comment on news, politics and world events.

Blogs can be used for recreation or in the workplace. They can be particularly valuable anywhere that people need to collaborate on an activity – from planning a wedding to running a political campaign. They can help keep everyone informed about project updates and are easier to use than a discussion forum.

If you want to create a blog, sign up with <u>www. blogger.com</u> where you can produce a simple Web log and have it stored on their hosting service. There is a small charge if you don't want to have adverts on your blog. Other useful information including links to award winning blogs can be found at <u>www.guardian.co.uk</u>.

Instant messaging

Instant messaging or chatting allows you to communicate in real-time (i.e. instantly) with another individual or a group of people over the Internet. There are several programs available which deliver instant messaging such as AOL's Instant Messenger, ICQ and MSN Messenger. However, note that if you have one of these programs you can only chat to people who also have the same program.

As well as chatting, MSN Messenger allows you to browse the Web together and see the same web pages, talk to one another directly via headsets and see one another through Web cameras (but this really needs a broadband connection to be effective). You can also send files or photos – the intended recipient gets to choose whether they want to receive anything before it is sent.

Choosing an Internet service

Assuming that you have a computer with browser software such as Internet Explorer, a modem and access to a telephone socket, you then just need to open an account with an Internet service provider to be able to go online. There is a wide choice of possible service providers from AOL to Freeserve to Virgin and your final decision will probably be based on cost, availability in your area and quality of service. Your first decision will be whether to opt for a dial-up connection or a faster broadband connection.

The time taken for a Web page to load onto your computer is partly determined by the **bandwidth** of your Internet connection. The wider the bandwidth, the more information that can pass and the faster Web pages will appear onscreen.

A **dial-up connection** provides the lowest bandwidth but is the cheapest option. In theory, a typical dial-up modem will operate at up to 56 kbps (kilobits per second); that is 56,000 bits transferred every second where 8 bits represents one letter or number. This might seem a lot but it will feel slow if you are viewing a Web page which as a lot of graphics.

A **broadband connection** is much faster than dial-up but broadband can mean anything from 128 kbps to 1000 kbps. Generally, the more bandwidth, the more it costs. There may also be a charge for the special broadband modem and a further charge to connect it – although some ISPs may waive these charges because competition can be fierce. You will also need to check whether broadband is available in your area.

If you want to watch film clips or music videos or play interactive games over the Internet then you should opt for broadband as dial-up connections were never designed for this level of use. However, if you are mainly going to use your Internet connection for email and websites where graphics are not important then a dial-up connection may well suffice.

Another factor to bear in mind is the use of your telephone. The phone line will not be available for voice calls when a dial-up modem is in use so if your household receives a lot of phone calls a dial-up modem may not be ideal. On the other hand, broadband has the advantage that the phone line is not affected. In addition, if you choose to, the broadband connection can be left on so any emails sent to you are received instantly – you do not have to log on and download them as with a dial-up connection.

If you decide that a dial-up modem is appropriate for your needs you can now choose between a Pay as You Go connection or unlimited access. With Pay as You Go you only pay for the use of your telephone line at something like 1 p per minute for the time that you are online. With unlimited access you pay a monthly fee of £10–£15 to connect to the Internet as often as you want at any time of day and there are no charges against your phone bill.

If you decide that broadband is what you need, you can expect to pay between £17.50 and £35 per month for the subscription which will give you fast and unlimited access to the Internet.

What to expect from an ISP

Once you have decided on the kind of service that you want there are a few other factors you should consider before choosing an ISP.

Online information services like America Online (AOL) provide additional content as well as a link to the Internet. This can include news, sport and entertainment channels or access to chat sessions. Expect to pay extra for these services.

Is there a free trial period to allow you to evaluate how easily you can access the Internet? If the ratio of users to modems at the ISP is more than about 8 to 1 then you may have difficulty connecting at peak times. It is also useful to find how helpful the helpline service is, the hours when it is available and how much it costs. Some telephone support lines charge £1 per minute.

Other features that may be of interest include: the number of email addresses available; advice and support with antivirus protection and safe surfing; the quality of any content provided; and the amount and nature of any advertising on the home page.

Finally, you can check reviews of ISPs in computer magazines and at Web sites such as ispreview.co.uk. According to ispreview, the UK's top ten ISPs (by number of subscribers) are as follows.

ISP NAME - Subscribers
1.Wanadoo (2,500,000)
2. AOL UK (2,300,000)
3. BTOpenworld (1,780,000)
4. Tiscali (1,694,000)
5. NTL (1,432,000)
6. Telewest BY (774,000)
7. Breathe (630,000)
8. Virgin (600,000)
9. Clara.net (450,000)
10. Brightview (400,000)

Updated: 16/01/2005

Getting connected

When you have chosen your ISP you next have to set up your connection. There are several ways to get connected. The most straightforward method uses an installation CD-ROM supplied by your ISP – just insert the disc and follow the instructions. The second method uses the New Connection wizard in Windows to take you through the steps involved. For both methods you will need to supply a user name and a password (although the latter may be provided for you initially). If you are setting up an account for other than a Pay as You Go service then you may need to supply credit card details as well. You may have to provide your credit card details even if you are trialling a service. You often have to actively cancel the service at the end of the trial if you do not want to continue using it.

If you use the Windows New Connection wizard to set up your connection you must first arrange your user name and password with the ISP who will also provide a dial-up phone number for you to enter on the appropriate screen.

Don't hesitate to phone the helpline at your ISP if you should run into problems trying to set up your account.

Once you have registered and set up your connection you are ready to go online. However, before doing so please ensure that you have installed antivirus software and a firewall. It would also be useful to have read the chapter on security which covers safety issues on the Web.

Using Internet Explorer

Internet Explorer is the Microsoft program which enables you to read, or browse, Web pages. To start Internet Explorer and go online, click on the Start button, point to Programs and click on Internet Explorer. A dialog box may then appear onscreen which gives you the option to Connect or to Work Offline. Alternatively, you may have to click on a button or shortcut which has been provided by your ISP and then follow any instructions that appear.

When you go online the first Web page that you see onscreen is your ISP's home page. A home page is like a contents page for a Web site with clickable **hyperlinks** to the pages inside and usually to external Web sites as well. The home page often has a row of links at the top of the page or a column at the side of the page (or both). You will also find links in the body of the text as well. These are often indicated by an underline or a change of text colour or the use of bold type. Any pictures or images that you see on a home page may also operate as links as well as being illustrations. If you are not sure whether an item is a link you can check by hovering over it with the mouse. The arrow should change to a pointing hand and a screen tip describing the link may also appear.

Before venturing further onto the Web here are some of the key features of Internet Explorer that you may find useful.

Menus

Internet Explorer has the usual Windows File, Edit and View menus together with one called Favorites which enables you to store links to frequently visited Web sites.

Fig. 7.4 Internet Explorer's menu bar and standard toolbar

Fig. 7.5 Internet Explorer's standard toolbar

You can use the File menu to open, save or print Web pages just as in Word. In addition, if you want to use Internet Explorer to view a saved Web page without going online then click File and choose Work Offline.

The Edit menu allows you to Select, Cut, Copy and Paste text or images from a Web page. It also includes the Find facility to help you locate text within a given Web page.

The View menu has several very useful features. Click View then Full Screen to remove all of the toolbars except the Standard Buttons from the screen to give priority to the content on the Web page. If the type onscreen is a bit too small to read you may be able to increase the size of type by clicking View then Text Size and choosing a larger size. Unfortunately, this does not work on all Web sites because it is dependent on how the Web site has been developed.

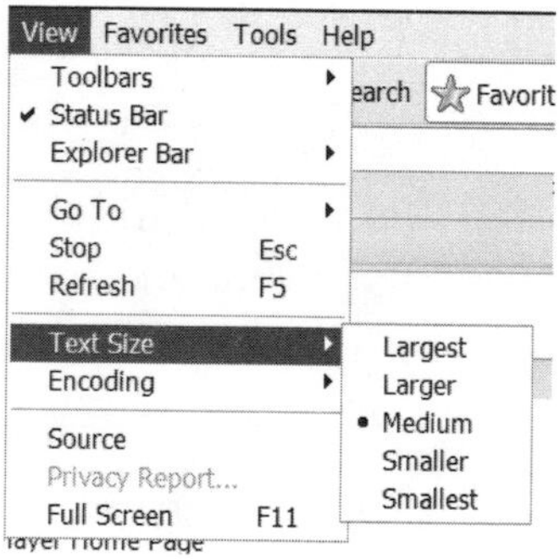

Fig. 7.6 Click View then point to Text Size to change the size of type on a web page

Click View then point to Toolbars to select the toolbars that you want onscreen. The main Standard Buttons include:

- **Back** – Use this if you click on a hyperlink that takes you to another Web page and you want to return to your original page. It will actually allow you to click back through the last nine Web pages that you visited.

Fig. 7.7 Back button

- **Forward** – Use this to 'retrace' your steps after having used the Back button.

Fig. 7.8 Forward button

- **Stop** – A well produced Web page should take no longer than 15 seconds to download to your computer on a dial-up connection. If you ever get fed up waiting and want to halt a page from loading, just click the Stop button.

Fig. 7.9 Stop button

- **Refresh** – If you are reading a fast-moving news item on the Web, clicking the Refresh button will display the latest version of the page.

Fig. 7.10 Refresh button

- **Home** – Clicking on the Home button will take you back to your home page.

Fig. 7.11 Home button

- **Search** – Opens the Explorer pane (see below) at the left of the screen into which you can type keywords that will help you to find relevant Web sites.

Fig. 7.12 Search button

- **Favorites** – Allows you to store the addresses of Web sites that you are likely to visit again. Clicking on the Favorites button switches the Explorer pane on at the left of the screen with links which you have saved so that you can reach them quickly.

Fig. 7.13 Favorites button

- **History** – lets you see all the Web sites that you have visited recently.

Fig. 7.14 History button

The **address bar** is one of the features of Internet

Explorer that you will use most often. This is where you key in the Web address of the site you want to visit. Technically the Web address is known as a **URL** (Uniform Resource Locator) and includes the string of characters **http://** as well as **www.** You will see these in the address bar but you don't need to type them if you are visiting a World Wide Web site as Internet Explorer includes them for you. If the address bar is not onscreen, click View and point to Toolbars and click on Address Bar.

Address 🔲 http://www.ntlworld.com/indexBroadband.php ✕ ➔ Go

Fig. 7.15 Address bar

It is a good idea to check that Status Bar is also selected in the View menu. If a Web page takes a long time to appear onscreen the status bar can provide useful clues to what is happening such as the number of images still to be downloaded.

The Explorer bar is a pane that can be opened at the left of the screen to display several options such as a search engine, your list of frequently visited Web sites (Favorites) and sites you have visited recently (History). Click View then point to Explorer to select the pane you want.

Clicking on View and pointing to GoTo gives you three navigation options: to go back a page, go forward a page or go to the home page. Most users probably find it more convenient to use the corresponding buttons on the toolbar. Likewise with the Stop and Refresh commands which can also be reached from the View menu.

The Favorites menu allows you to save the URLs of Web sites that you visit frequently and to organise them in folders if you wish. To add a link to Favorites, click Favorites then Add to Favourites. The following dialog box appears.

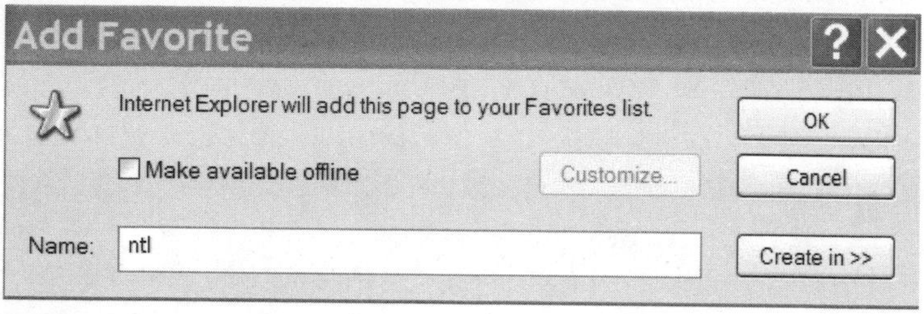

Fig. 7.16 Add to Favorites dialog box

If you cannot see the Create in area, click the Create in button and you should then see a list with some folders. If your URL is one that you use very frequently consider putting it in the Links folder as it will then appear in the Links toolbar. Alternatively, make sure Favorites is selected in the Create in box, paste the URL into the Name box and click OK. (It should appear automatically if you are working online.) Once you have a few entries in Favorites you can create folders and organise your links into categories if you wish.

You can also add links to Favorites and organise them into folders by clicking the Favorites button on the toolbar. This opens the Explorer toolbar at the side with the Favorites option selected. Click Add to include a link then paste the URL into the Name box.

When organising your Favorites you can cut and paste or click and drag the links between folders as you can with files.

From the Tools menu you can open Outlook Express by clicking Mail and News and choosing Read Mail. You can also check to see if there are any recent updates to Windows available for downloading by clicking Windows Update.

Show Related Links is a facility which suggests alternative Web sites to the one you are presently viewing.

Clicking on Tools then Options brings up the Internet Options window which can also be reached from the Control Panel. (Click on Start, Settings, Control Panel.) The options available here give you some control over your security and privacy when surfing the Web.

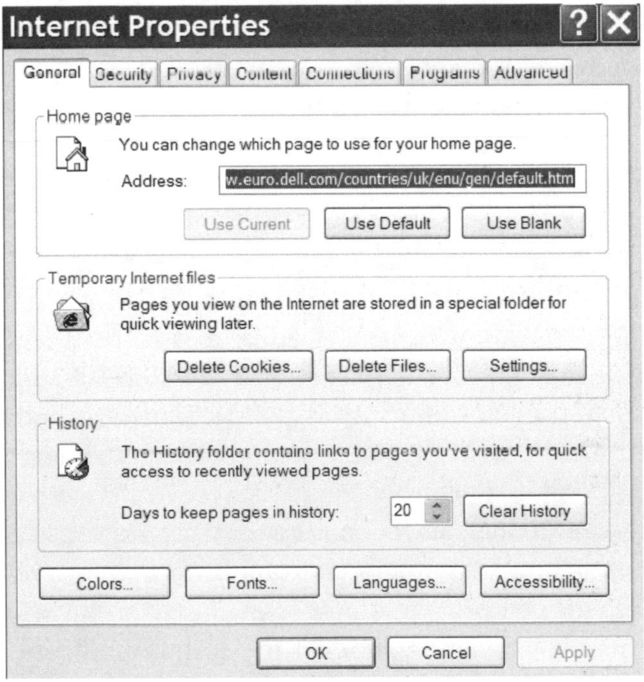

Fig. 7.17 Internet options General tab

General

On the General tab under Home Page you have the option to change your home page from that of your Internet service provider. To select a page from the Web, you first have to go to the Web page then click Use Current, then Apply and finally OK to complete the change. If you don't want to use any page as a home page, click on Use Blank instead of Use current.

The second category on the General tab is temporary Internet files. These are copies of the Web pages that you visit and they are stored on your computer so that the pages load faster the next time that you visit them. The Temporary Internet Files folder where the files are stored is sometimes referred to as the **cache**. If you find that you have thousands of files for sites that you no longer visit you can remove them by clicking Delete Files. You can also minimise the space that the next lot of files take up by clicking on Settings and reducing the slider on the 'Amount of disk space to use' scale to a minimum.

The first button shown under the temporary Internet files heading is Delete Cookies. A **cookie** is a small text file that is placed on your hard disk by a Web site. They store information about your computer and which pages you have visited so that the Website can recognise you the next time that you visit and possibly suggest pages or items that you might want to look at. If you register with a site and complete an online form the details will be stored on a cookie so that you can be 'personally' welcomed to the site the next time you visit. If you want to see how sophisticated this customisation software can be go to www.amazon.co.uk. The only Web site that can access a cookie is the one that places it on your machine. However, see the section below that covers the privacy tab to see why you may want to use the Delete Cookies option from time to time.

The third button under Temporary Internet Files is the settings button. Click on this to specify how much disk space you want to use to store temporary Internet files and how frequently you want Internet Explorer to check for updated versions of stored pages.

The third area under the General tab is History. This is where you can specify how long you want to keep a record of the Web sites you have visited and where you can clear the records altogether if you wish.

Privacy and more about cookies

Before supplying personal information such as your name and email address to a Website always check to see that the Web site has a privacy policy and check it to see how they will use your information. Look for a commitment to maintaining your privacy such as in the site below. Be cautious about sites that share your information with 'trusted partners' particularly if you do not know the organisation which runs the site. Before you know it you could be just one more recipient of spam email.

Cookies can be temporary or persistent. A temporary cookie is removed from your computer when you finish a session and close Internet Explorer. A persistent cookie could remain on your machine for years unless you delete it.

If you visit a Web site that has adverts, often an ad will actually be on another Web site without you being aware of it and the advertising agency's server will send you a cookie (referred to as a third-party cookie) without you even clicking on the advert. If you then go to another Web page that has adverts from the same agency the advertising agency can track your movements and build up a profile of you. The profile will normally be anonymous and your data combined with that of other users. However,

cookies can supply information about you to others without you necessarily realising that you were providing it!
To take control of cookies, go to the Privacy tab.

Privacy tab

The Privacy tab lets you choose the kind of cookie that
will be allowed onto your machine. Move the slider up
and down to see the various options.

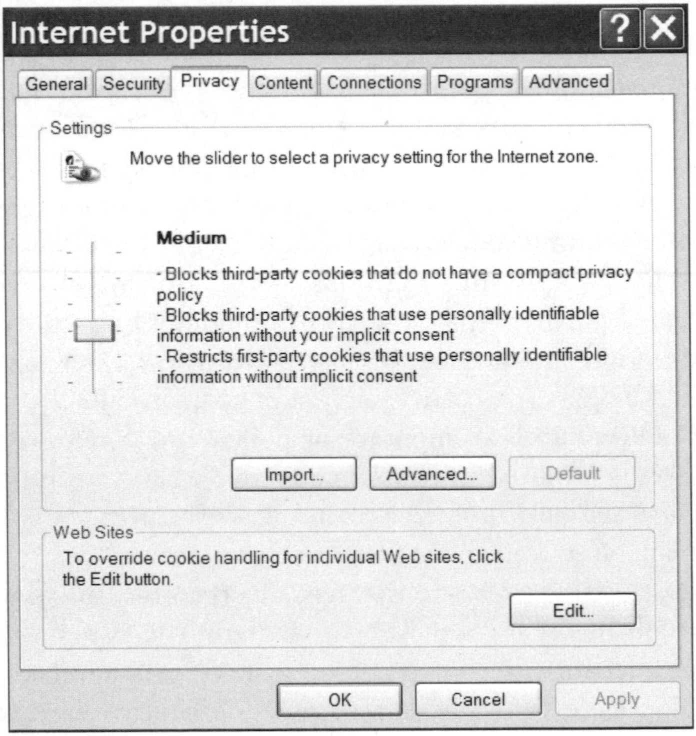

Fig 7.18 Privacy tab

The top setting of the scale blocks any new cookies
from being added to your machine and prevents any

cookies already present from being read. However, some Web sites demand that you allow cookies before you can view them. For example, the technical support site www.mcafeehelp.co.uk requires you to enable cookies before you can use their Help service.

When the slider is set to High, cookies from Web sites that do not have a privacy policy that can be read by your computer (a compact privacy policy) are automatically blocked. In addition, cookies from Web sites which 'use your personally identifiable information without your explicit consent' are also blocked.

When set to Medium High, cookies from third-party Web sites that do not have a compact policy are blocked. This means that cookies from advertisers that have a privacy policy *will* be allowed onto your machine. However, cookies from third-party Web sites that 'use your personally identifiable information without your *explicit* consent' are blocked. However, note that only cookies from first-party Web sites which 'use your personally identifiable information without your *implicit* consent' are blocked. Here the key word is *implicit*. Does just visiting the site imply that you have given implicit consent? There are two actions you can take. Firstly, always read the privacy policy before you provide any personal information. Secondly, to check whether a site adheres to its published policy, look for a symbol such as the TRUSTe symbol shown below.

Fig 7.19 The TRUSTe logo

At Medium setting, cookies from third-party Web sites that do not have a compact policy are still blocked, as are third-party Web sites that use your personally identifiable information without your *implicit* consent. Finally, cookies from first-party Web sites that use personally identifiable information without implicit consent are deleted when Internet Explorer is closed.

On the Low setting, cookies from third-party Web sites that do not have a compact policy are blocked but third-party Web sites that use your personally identifiable information are allowed but are deleted when you close Internet Explorer.

The final setting is Accept all cookies – which means what it says!

To set the privacy setting that you have selected, click Apply then OK. Privacy settings only relate to Web sites in the Internet zone.

Security tab

The Security tab allows you to set different security levels for different Web sites. It does this by providing four separate security zones as shown in the diagram below. The Internet zone will probably be the only one that you use, at least initially.

To set a security level while you are on the Internet, click on the Internet icon and then move the slider to an appropriate level. The default setting is Medium. If you choose a setting lower than Medium you run a risk of spyware programs (see Security chapter) being downloaded onto your computer without your knowledge. If you choose the High setting you may not see some animated features on some Websites.

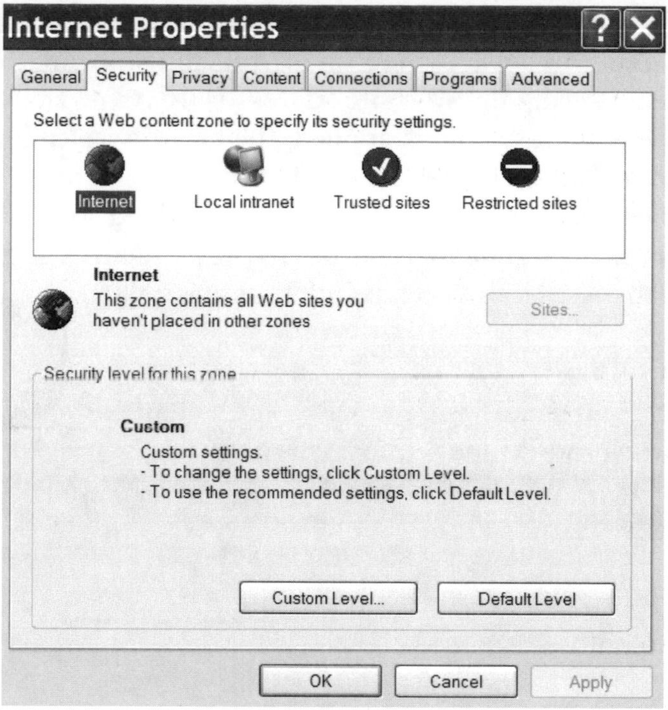

Fig. 7.20 Internet options Security tab

The Medium setting states that 'Unsigned ActiveX controls will not be downloaded'. ActiveX is type of program that was developed by Microsoft that can add interactivity, including animation, to Web sites. If an ActiveX control is signed there will be a certificate indicating who created the control and you can then choose whether to trust it. An unsigned control has no certificate. The other zone options available are: Local Intranet, Trusted Sites and Restricted Sites. An intranet is a private network which many organisations have. If your employer has an intranet the security level will have been set by the IT department.

If you trust a particular site you can add it to the Trusted Sites zone by clicking the icon then clicking the Sites button and keying the Web site address (URL) into the box. If the default setting is applied, the security setting will then be Low whenever you visit this site.

Sites which you do not trust can be added to the Restricted Sites zone in the same way. The security setting will then be High if the default option is selected.

Content tab

The Content tab has three sections: Content Advisor, Certificates and Personal Information.

Fig. 7.21 Internet options content tab

You can use Content Advisor to set controls for language, nudity, sex and violence. Each category has a sliding scale from zero (none) to four (explicit/gratuitous) but click the More Info button to link to the ratings service which filters the content. You can change bureaus by clicking on the Ratings button on the General tab.

Under the Approved sites tab you can approve sites or block them and under the General tab you can set a password to control amendments to this list.

If you are a parent and content is a concern for you please do not expect content filters to be 100 per cent effective – web sites can have false ratings. In addition, note that not every site has a rating so if you allow unrated sites (General tab) you should be aware that some may contain adult content.

Certificates let you confirm your identity when you visit a Website or let you check on the security of a Web site.

The Personal Information section has two features: Autocomplete and My Profile. If AutoComplete is switched on it will suggest possible entries when you start typing a Web address for a Web site that you have visited before. Similarly it will indicate possible entries for online forms including usernames and passwords if you wish. Click the Autocomplete button to switch these options on or off and to clear the form completion and password histories.

My Profile is intended to save you time whenever you are asked by a Web site for your name or email address. Your profile is stored on your machine but cannot be seen by others or transmitted to a Web Site without your permission. To create a profile, click on the My Profile button then select 'Create a new entry in the address book to represent your profile' and click OK. Be aware that if you complete all the options you will be providing a lot of information about yourself. Also, if you prefer, you do not need to use this feature at all.

Searching the World Wide Web

There are several ways in which you can look for information on the Web. If you know the Web address of a particular site that you have in mind, you can go online and key the URL into the Internet Explorer address bar and press Enter. Alternatively, if you do not know the site name, your ISP's home page will probably offer various channels with links to sport, news, entertainment and other Web sites from which you can click on hyperlinks until you find what ever you are looking for. However, you could spend a lot of time 'surfing' until you find what you want. A much faster way is to use a search engine or a subject directory.

A search engine is a program that uses software robots called spiders to 'crawl' about the Web from site to site looking for keywords that describe the content of a particular site. This information is then stored in a database and when a user subsequently uses the search engine by typing in a keyword, a selection of the Web pages in the database where the keyword appears are displayed onscreen. Entries higher up the list match the search criteria better than those further down. To try to ensure that the most worthwhile pages receive prominence in the list, the search engine Google also looks at the number of links into a site from other sites as this is an indication of site popularity.

Most ISPs provide a search engine on the home page or you can use the default search engine through Internet Explorer by clicking on the Search button on the toolbar. The toolbar opens on the left of the screen with a box for you to type in one or more keywords.

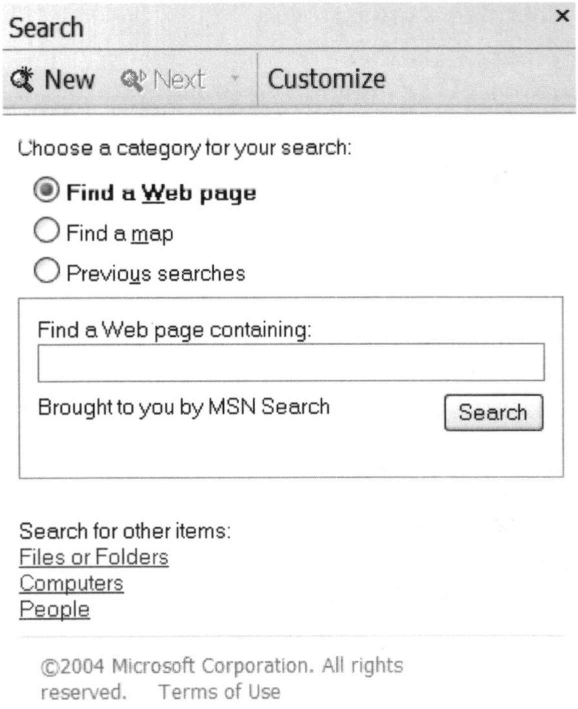

Fig. 7.22 Search pane showing IE default search engine

The choice of words is important when using a search engine. If you search on the word 'music' the search engine will indicate millions of hits covering everything from classical to world music. You can narrow down the selection by combining words. For example, if you are interested in Gaelic bagpipe music you would key in:

Music +Gaelic + bagpipe

The search engine will then find pages which contain instances of these words.

If you are looking for Gaelic music but cannot stand bagpipes then use a minus sign instead:

Music +Gaelic –bagpipe

Search engines often miss out words like 'the' and 'of' so if these are important, for example perhaps they appear in the title of a song, then put the whole title within double quotation marks:

"Bright side of the road"

If the word that you are searching for can have several endings you can try just putting the stem of the word with an asterisk as a **wild card**. For example,

Vocal*

should bring up references to: vocals, vocalist and vocalists in a search engine like Google but note that many search engines do not have this feature.

When searching the Web remember that words often have more than one meaning and that there are sites out there on all sorts of topics that do not claim to be wholesome family viewing. So if you are looking for a good price for a new television you might find more than you bargained for if you key in 'TV offers'. The safer surfing section of the Security chapter provides guidance on how to avoid unwelcome surprises.

Search engines to try

www.google.co.uk/

Google is currently the flavour of the month as far as search engines are concerned. It searches over 8 billion Web pages and is very fast and easy to use. After you have typed in your keyword you can choose to search just UK sites or the whole Web. There is also an 'I'm Feeling Lucky' button which automatically opens the page that appears at the top of the search list.

On Google, each Web page is given a PageRank which is a tally of the number of links into a page from other pages across the Web. Consequently, the sites listed by Google appear in an order of popularity – which is useful for Google users because if a particular page has multiple links into it probably contains useful content. None of the positions in the list are as a result of organisations paying to appear near the top. Google does have what it refers to as sponsored sites but these appear separately either towards the right-hand side of the screen or above the main listing.

You also will not find any pop-up advertisements on Google. In fact, if you download the Google toolbar and activate its pop-up blocker it will stop pop-ups appearing on pages that you subsequently visit.

You can personalise Google by clicking on Preferences where there are various language options to choose from and you can also choose a safe surfing option to avoid the possible listing of sites with potentially offensive material.

Google has a Directory in addition to the Web search facility. You browse through various categories and sub-categories until you find the topic you want. Google then provides a list of relevant Web sites which have been reviewed by an editor. This task is carried out by over 20,000 editors who volunteer their time to the Open Directory Project. To find out how to become an editor, click on the Become an editor link at the foot of every Directory page.

Next to the Directory button on the home page is the News button. Google's news service searches over 4500 news sources and organises them into the following categories: Top stories, World, UK (if you select the .co.uk site in Preferences), Business, Science and Technology, Entertainment and Health. Each entry provides a link to the source of the article and states when it was posted so that you can see how current it is. There are also links to related stories and if you cannot find a particular topic you can of course search the news pages for it.

Google also provides a range of other services including Google Images (an index to over 425 million images) and Google groups (an archive of Usenet discussion groups with over 700 million posts going all the way back to 1981). To see a full listing of what Google has to offer, click on Tools and Services.

Yahoo!

Yahoo! began as a directory in which the entries which appeared in its index were all compiled by people. It now uses Google's search engine to supplement this directory service. However, the usefulness of having someone check and list entries is still valid because searching for a specialised subject on Google may not produce the required results.

AltaVista (http://uk.altavista.com/)

AltaVista is an innovative search engine. It provides a directory, news, images, audio and video categories as well as its Web search function. Its forte is multilingual provision and the Babel Fish translator (http://babelfish.altavista.com/) will translate up to 150 words at a time between 19 pairs of languages. AltaVista advises that Babel Fish is intended to help you 'grasp the general intent of the original' and that you should not expect a 'polished translation'.

MSN Search (http://uk.search.msn.com/)

MSN Search is usually the default search engine for Internet Explorer. It is family oriented in that it avoids sites which specialise in adult content.

A **meta-search engine** searches other search engines instead of the Web and then compiles what it takes to be the most relevant results. A meta-search engine can lead to more up-to-date results compared to using a single search engine and since each search engine follows different criteria when gathering results a meta-search engine can reduce the chance of a useful find slipping through the net.

Dogpile UK (http://www.dogpile.co.uk/)

Dogpile is an example of a meta-search engine. Dogpile.co.uk returns results from Google, Yahoo, AltaVista, Overture, Mirago, Teoma, WebFinder and Espotting.

Info.co.uk (http://www.info.co.uk/)

Info.co.uk is another example of a meta-search engine. It covers Google, Ask Jeeves, Thomson Webfinder, Yahoo, Altavista, Fast, Ask Jeeves, Looksmart, Overture, E-Spotting and Open Directory.

Evaluating what you find on the Web

You have found a search engine that you like and you have typed in a keyword which has returned a list of suggested Web sites. What should you look for on a Web site to enable you to evaluate whether it will be usable, trustworthy and provide information that meets your needs?

Step 1

Check what any summary wording on the search engine listing actually states. It is not unknown for porn sites to masquerade as something completely different. What looks like a site that provides road maps round Europe may actually be delivering a service of a completely different kind. The search engine summary wording is the first clue that you will get as to what a site might be like.

Step 2

When you click on the search engine link and arrive at the requested page, be aware that this might not be the home page of the site. Any reasonably constructed site will have a link to its home page on every single page. Sometimes the link will be an organisational logo but ideally there should be a text hyperlink as well.

Open the home page and look for a description of the purpose of the site and who is responsible for the site. Look for a button or a link called 'About Us' or something similar. Click on this link and check how much information the sponsor of the site is prepared to give you about themselves. Is there a name, address, phone number and email address? Sometimes this information may appear under a 'Contact' link.

Step 3

Try to gauge the breadth and depth of the site content. What links are provided in the site's navigation bars? Is there a site map? A site map is the equivalent of a contents page of a book and lets you see at a glance the topics which are covered throughout the site and the way in which the site is structured.

Step 4

Consider the quality of the site. Does the overall design have a professional look and feel? Are there any spelling or factual errors? Is there a search facility or a help feature? When was the site last updated? Watch out for the cheats which rather than really showing when the site was updated show today's date! Is there any bias in the information provided? Who has ownership of the site?

Step 5

If the site has advertisements are they obviously separate from the main content? Try running a search on Google to see an example of non-intrusive advertising. Check to see if the site has a privacy policy which clearly states that it will not sell your personal information to anyone or pass it to anyone other than individuals or organisations that are required to deliver the service that the Web site provides. When you visit a Web site your browser informs the server of your email address. A less than scrupulous Web site may record your email addresses without you knowing and sell it to a spammer.

Printing Web pages

If you want to print out a Web page, click File then Print. A dialog box then appears and if the Web site is constructed using frames to group the various items of content on the screen you will have three options. You can print the page just as it is laid out on the screen or you can print just one selected frame or all the frames individually. If you want to you can print out all the pages which are linked to the current page or just a table of links to those pages by selecting the appropriate check box.

Saving text and images from the Web

If you find a useful article on the Web and want to save it on to your machine for reference later you can save the Web page as a whole by clicking File then Save As and storing it as a Web page in an appropriate folder. However, this will also capture the navigation bars, adverts and other possibly superfluous items on the page. If you just want the text and some relevant images proceed as follows. Select the text that you want then click Edit and Copy. Next, open a new Word document and paste your selection into it. Finally, save the Word document in your preferred folder.

The last option retains any original formatting in the text. If you would prefer not to have this, try copying your selection into Notepad first. This removes all formatting including that of tables but you have 'clean' text which can then be cut and pasted into a Word document.

If you are likely to want to go back to the Web page where you found the article or if you are a student and need to be able to cite the source, it is worthwhile selecting and copying the URL of the Web page into your Word document and noting the date when you down loaded it. Web pages often change frequently or may be removed without warning.

Saving an image from a Web page is similarly straightforward. Right click on the image that you require then click on Save Picture As. A dialog box opens so that you can choose the folder where you want to keep the image.

Downloading files

Web sites sometimes provide files that can be downloaded in portable document format which can be recognised by the file extension .pdf. The advantage of PDF files to the user is that they can be opened on Macintosh computers and PCs alike and you do not need to have the software that created the original file in order to view them. There are several advantages to the provider of the information: they only have to supply one file that fits all rather than several customised files; the file will display the document with the layout and font styles that the designer intended; and the creator of the pdf can lock it to prevent the document from being altered easily.

In order to open and view a pdf file you need to first install Adobe Reader which is a free program from Adobe Systems. Usually a Web site that provides pdf files will have a link to the Adobe site so that you can download Acrobat Reader – look for the Get Acrobat icon. Alternatively, go to http://www.adobe.co.uk/products/acrobat/readstep2.html and follow the instructions.

Once you have Adobe Reader is installed on your machine it will open automatically whenever you double click on a pdf icon on a Web site. You can then choose whether to view the pdf online or to save it to your hard disk.

The disadvantage of pdf files is that you cannot readily amend them without the full Adobe Acrobat program which can be a nuisance if you don't have the full program and need to complete a job application where the form is only available as a pdf. What you can do however, is key in your application details in Adobe Reader then print out the application – however, you will not be able to save an electronic version so you need to make sure that the application is complete and correct before closing the pdf file. You can also copy text from a pdf into a Word document where you can amend it. Click on the Text tool to enable you to select the required text then press Control and C at the same time and paste the selection into a Word document. Note that the formatting of any tables will be lost when you do this and it will not work if the pdf has been locked.

If you do copy text or images from the Web remember that you are legally obliged to respect the copyright owner's rights. Look for a copyright statement on the Web page. You may be entitled to copy and use material for individual use as long as it is not for profit and you acknowledge the copyright owner, but do not automatically assume this.

Adobe Reader is a type of program that is often referred to as a plug-in. The term is used for any small program that 'plugs in' to another program such as to enable certain files to be opened that could not otherwise be accessed through the main program. Other examples of plug-in include Macromedia's Flash Player which enables animations that have been created in Flash to be displayed and Shockwave which is used for interactive games and to play streaming audio as used for Internet radio.

File Transfer Protocol (FTP)

When you download a file over the Internet the file is not sent as one huge block but is separated into small packets of data which are then moved sequentially from the server to your machine. The rules governing how the data is sent, and then checked at the receiving end, are known as a File Transfer Protocol. Internet Explorer uses a file transfer protocol when you download files from the Web. There are also other FTP client programs that can be used to download or upload files to FTP sites where files are exchanged.

Chapter 8
Microsoft Outlook Express

Introduction to email

When you sign up with an ISP you will be given an email account and an email address. All you then need is an email client program such as Outlook Express in order to receive and send emails. Outlook Express has many of the features of Outlook and is available free.

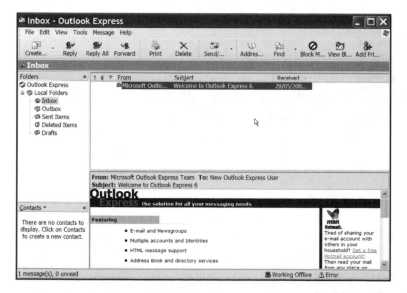

Fig. 8.1 Outlook Express Window

To send an email, you first start Outlook Express by clicking on the Start button, pointing to Programs and clicking on Outlook Express. Depending on your set-up, a dialog box may then appear which gives you the option to Connect or to Work Offline. If you have a dial-up connection you may prefer to compose your email offline.

You will then see a window which looks like that on the previous page.

Like other Microsoft programs, Outlook Express has the familiar Windows' File, Edit, View, Tools and Help menus plus an additional Message menu. Below this is the Outlook Express toolbar. Most of the screen space is taken up by the message pane which in this example shows email messages that have arrived in the Inbox. To the left of the message pane is the folder list which includes folders for the Inbox, Outbox, Sent Items, Deleted Items and Drafts.

A new message is started by clicking the Create Mail button then adding the email address of the person or organisation which is going to receive the email. The email address will have the following form:

jsmith@internetprovider.com

The message is also given a subject title or description. Once the message has been keyed in, and been checked, you click the Send/Receive button and the message moves to your Outbox. If you are working offline, the message will remain here until you next connect to your ISP.

When a message is sent it goes to the mail server at

your ISP and at the same time a copy of the message is placed in your Sent Items folder. The message then travels over the Internet until it reaches the mail server indicated in the email address and from there it is forwarded to the recipient's Inbox.

Using Outlook Express to send and receive email messages

It's called 'Outlook Express' so to get you started quickly here is one way to send and receive email messages.

1. Open Outlook Express from the Start menu or click the Outlook Express icon in the Quick launch toolbar.

Fig. 8.2 Outlook Express icon

2. Click the Create Mail button to open a New Message Window.

Fig. 8.3 Create Mail button

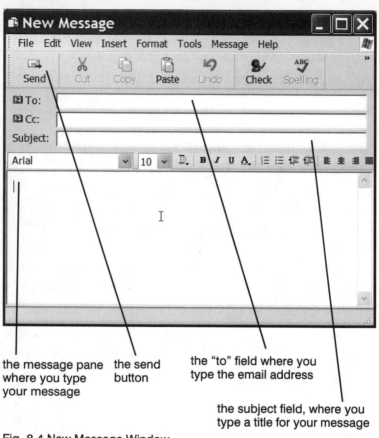

Fig. 8.4 New Message Window

3. Type the email address of the person you are sending the message to in the 'To' field where the insertion point is flashing. If you are sending the message to more than one person type a semicolon after each address.

4. Click on the Subject field and type in a title for your message.

5. Click on the message pane and type in your message.

6. Click the Send button. If you are currently connected to the Internet your message will be moved to the Outbox and then immediately sent to the mail server at your ISP. If you are working offline the message will be sent to your outbox and be held there until you next go online.

7. Click the Send/Receive button on the Outlook Express toolbar and any messages which were being held for you at your ISP will be forwarded to your Inbox. Click on Inbox in the folder list to see any messages which have been sent to you. (If you cannot see a folder list, click the View menu then click on Layout and make sure the Folder list option is ticked. Click Apply and then OK to complete the procedure.)

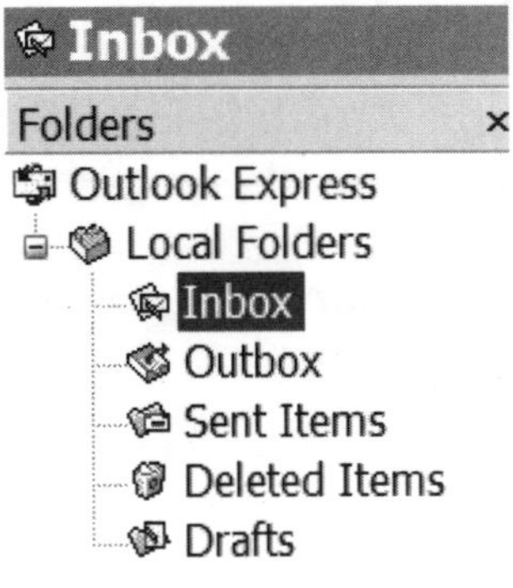

Fig. 8.5 Outlook Express folder list

8. To read a message, just double click it to open it – but read the next section first!

Attachments

You can attach files to your email messages. If you have your cv as a Word file you could attach it to an email message to apply for a job online. Alternatively, if you have a digital camera or a scanner you could send copies of your holiday snaps to your friends. Most types of file can be attached to email messages and here is how to do it.

Create a message in the usual way then click on the attach button on the toolbar.

Fig. 8.6 Attach button

A dialog box entitled Insert Attachment opens. Click through the folders until you find the file that you want. Click on the file then click Attach.

If you now look at the Attach field underneath the subject field on your message you should see the filename and the file size. If the file that you are sending is larger than 500 kB and you intend to send it to someone with a 56 kB dial-up connection then think twice about sending it as it could take a long time to download. You may even find that your ISP, or the recipient's ISP, automatically rejects attachment sizes greater than 1 MB.

If you are sent an email with a file attached you will see a paper clip icon alongside the message in your inbox. It is straightforward to open but before you do – 'think virus?'

A word of caution!

Viruses are often sent as email attachments. If you inadvertently open an attachment that is a virus without an antivirus program automatically scanning every file that you open you could find that the virus then sends copies of itself to every address in your address book. Please never ever open an attachment without an up-to-date antivirus program running – even if it is from someone you know as they could easily have been infected by a virus themselves.

Always check the file extension of the attachment. If it ends in .exe, .com or .vbs check that the sender meant to send it and ask what it is and where it was created. If you have any doubts about the original source of the file delete it without opening it. If you think that this is being over-cautious check out the security chapter to see the problems that viruses can produce.

If you do not know who sent the message and the description in the subject field is minimal (e.g. Hi!) or looks a bit suspicious then again consider deleting the message. Virus writers try to trick you into opening their attachments in all sorts of ways. The Love bug virus used the subject line 'I love you' while the My Doom virus purported to be a failed email delivery message.

Handling messages
Replying

Fig. 8.7 Reply button

If you have received a message and want to reply to it, click the Reply button at the left of the message toolbar to respond to the person who sent the message. Outlook Express creates a new message with the 'To:' field already completed because it knows who sent you the message. It also changes the subject field by adding 'Re:' at the start to indicate that this message is a response and it also includes the text of the original message. You then type in your message above the previous message. You can either delete the wording of the original message or leave it as a reminder to the person who sent it.

If the original message was sent to a number of people and you want to let them all see your reply then clicking the Reply to All button will create a reply message with all the relevant addresses in the 'To:' field.

If you want to copy the message to someone else but want to signal that you do not expect them to reply or take any action then include their address in the 'cc:' field.

Forwarding

Fig. 8.8 Forward button

Click the Forward button to send a message that you have received to someone else. A new message like a Reply is created but this time you have to type in the forwarding address in the 'To:' field. If you want to you can then add your own message above the original message before clicking the Send button.

Deleting messages

✕
Delete

Fig. 8.9 Delete button

The quickest way to delete a message after you have read it is to click the Delete button on the toolbar while the message is still open. The message will be moved to the Deleted Items folder which like the Recycle Bin retains deleted files until you empty the folder or restore the files.

Very soon, however, you will find that your inbox fills up with messages – some of which you might find useful to keep but there will be many others which are no longer required or which you don't want to read in the first place and which just take up disk space. To delete a single message, click on it to highlight it then press the Delete button. The message will be moved to the Deleted Items folder. To permanently delete a file you have to right click on the Deleted Items folder and choose Empty Deleted Items folder. You will then be asked if you want to permanently delete the items in the folder.

If you try to delete messages but find that nothing happens it may be that your messages are actually held on the server at your ISP and that you have to go online to remove them.

Saving messages in folders

You can create folders to store your messages in Outlook Express in the same way that you create folders in Windows.

Right click Local Folders on the folder list. The Create Folder dialog box opens from which you can choose where to place the new folder and give it a name. Once you have done this, click OK and the new folder appears in alphabetical order in the folder list. Repeat this process until you have all the folders that you need.

All you now have to do is click, drag and drop the emails in your Inbox to the appropriate folder. If the emails in your Inbox are held at your ISP, click Edit then Purge deleted messages to clear your Inbox.

Here are some other features of Outlook Express that you may find useful.

Menus

Click File then New to create new email, newsgroup or instant messages. You can also open, save or print emails from the File menu just as in Word. In addition, if you want to use Outlook Express to first compose an email before going online to send it, then click File and choose Work Offline.

The Edit menu allows you to Select, Copy and delete messages. It also lets you mark messages as read or unread and there is a Find facility to help you locate emails within your filing system. You can also use the Find feature to find people and businesses via an Internet directory service.

The View menu lets you organise the outlook Express Window. Click View then point to Current View to choose whether you want to Show All Messages or to Hide Read Messages.

Click View then Columns to select which columns you want to Show or Hide on screen. You can choose to display the Subject of a message, who a message was From or when it was Received and several other options then click View, Sort By to arrange messages alphabetically by column.

Click View then Layout to select the toolbars that you want onscreen and to choose whether or not to show messages in the preview pane. The preview pane can be useful because it lets you see part of the message as soon as it arrives in your Inbox. However, to do this it has to open the message. It is safer to keep the Show Preview Pane option unchecked in case you receive an email with a virus attached that can automatically launch itself when the email is opened.

To send or receive messages, click Tools and point to Send and Receive then choose one of three options. Clicking Send and Receive All will send any messages in your Outbox and download any that are waiting to be forwarded to you by your ISP. Alternatively, if you have nothing to send you can choose Receive All or if you have had enough email for the moment but want to send a message then click Send All.

If you end up receiving large quantities of email you can use the Message Rules feature to help deal with it efficiently. Click Tools then point to Message Rules and choose Email. You can then choose to automatically sort messages into specific folders, forward, delete or flag them.

You can also access the address book, Windows Messenger and Newsgroups from the Tools menu as well as add and remove mail and newsgroup accounts and choose various options as to how your mail is handled.

Finally, you can use the Message menu to create new emails and to reply to emails or to forward them to others.

Address book

Outlook Express includes an address book which you can use to store and manage the contact details of everyone that you communicate with. You can store home and work addresses, phone numbers, birthdays, nicknames and of course email addresses. To add a contact's email address just right click on it in a message and choose Add to Contacts.

To add other details to the address book, click on the Address Book button on the toolbar to open the Address Book window then click on the New button and choose New Contact then fill in the fields that you want to use.

Addre...

Fig. 8.10 Address Book button

You can open new messages from the Address Book that are pre-addressed by selecting a contact then clicking on the Action button and Choosing Send Mail. You can also group email addresses so that they appear as one entry in the address book. This can be handy if, say, you want to send a message to all your friends that are interested in a particular pastime, or to work colleagues or to close family and so on. Click the New button then choose New Group. The Group Properties dialog box opens. Click on

Select to select the members of the group and then give the group a name. After you click OK the group name will be included in the folder list of the Address Book.

Identities

If you look at the title bar of your Address Book it may indicate that it is the address book for the main identity. Outlook Express allows you to have more than one identity. For example, if you have run a business you might want to keep your business identity separate from the identity you use when posting to a Star Trek newsgroup.

To give yourself a new identity, go to the main Outlook Express menu and click File then point to Identities and click Add New Identity. In the dialog box which appears type your new name. You are asked if you want to switch identities immediately then the Manage Identities dialog box opens where you can then create another identity or delete a previous one.

Once you have set up your new identity it is straightforward to switch. Just click File then Switch Identities and choose the option you want.

Netiquette

Netiquette is the term that has been coined for etiquette when you are online. It is an important aspect of email for the following reasons.

1. Email messages need to be as clear as possible to avoid

misunderstandings. Always go to extra lengths to make sure that your wording is as clear as possible and be very careful of humour unless the person you are emailing knows you very well. That witty sarcasm which you occasionally use with your mates could be completely misconstrued if you allow it into your email messages while at work.

2. The explanation mark has always been used for emphasis or to convey emotion but the online world has taken the technique to new levels (or possibly depths!) with the development of emoticons. The smiley emoticon is one that is frequently used to denote that you are pleased or happy about something and is made up of a colon followed by a closing bracket like this :) If you are working in a recent version of Word you may find that your emoticon is converted by the AutoCorrect feature into a symbol like this ☺, ☻, ☹ . The table below lists some of the emoticons that you may come across.

:-)   smiling
:o)   alternative smiley
:-D   big smile
:-O   surprised
:-*   kiss
;-)   winking
:-(unhappy
:'-(crying
:-| blank expression
*<:o)   clowning around
c_/   cup of coffee/tea
:-(*)   feeing sick

Another technique which is sometimes used to clarify meaning is the use of words or phrases within angle brackets, for example <wink> would indicate that something was not meant to be taken seriously.

However, note that if you type a message in capital letters it means that you are SHOUTING! So watch that Caps lock key in case you cause offence.

3. Be careful what you write in case it comes back to haunt you. It is not unknown for personal messages to have been intercepted and forwarded to so many people that you might as well have made an announcement on television. A message sent to a work email could be read by a nosy colleague of the recipient, an IT administrator or a manager.

   Likewise take care that you address an email properly. It is a nuisance to receive someone else's email but you might be putting yourself at risk if your email goes to a complete stranger at "mailto:joe.bloggs@isp.com" joe.bloggs@isp.com instead of j.bloggs@isp.com .

4. When you reply to an email the original message is included below your message for reference. If you get involved in a protracted conversation by email this 'thread' of messages can become quite long. If you think it might be a good idea to then forward the final email to someone else for information then you might not be making yourself very popular. It would be a lot more considerate to re-present the information in the email instead of expecting the recipient to work through the thread. In addition, the longer an email is the longer it

takes to download and you could be costing someone time and possibly money if the have a dial-up connection.

5. Although email can travel great distances in fractions of a second, sometimes it can get 'stuck' in the system particularly if the network is being affected by a virus outbreak. So don't assume that your message will be read straight away and even more so if it was sent to a computer with a dial-up connection.

   If you don't go online for a while, such as when you are on holiday for example, you may find a lot of email in your inbox the next time that you connect. If there is more than one email from the same person it is a good idea to read all their messages before responding as a later email may supersede an earlier one.

6. Think before you address an email particularly if you are at work. If you copy or forward an email to a work colleague and it is likely to be only of marginal interest to them then think twice about including them – particularly if they are one of the unfortunate many that can receive over a hundred emails a day. On the other hand, you can inadvertently cause offence if you miss someone off an email address list so it can pay not to rush this procedure.

Spam

Spam is unsolicited (usually commercial) email. Spam often advertises get-rich-quick schemes, prescription drugs, loans, online qualifications or porn. According to some experts, if you have an email address it will only be a matter of time before you receive your first unwanted piece of spam.

Most suppliers of antivirus software also sell spam blocking software. However, they will not stop all spam getting through and they may even block legitimate mail. So how can you reduce your potential exposure to spam? A clue lies in the way in which spammers collect email addresses. There are two main ways.

Dictionary attacks use programs to generate likely email addresses which are then sent an email. Messages sent to addresses that don't exist get returned but the others are delivered. The worst thing that you can do is to respond to such a message. Asking to be removed from a spam mail list just lets the sending computer know that your email address is a live one and you are likely to receive yet more unwanted correspondence.

The second method is through the use of spiders or Web crawlers which trawl through Web sites and newsgroup listings for email addresses. If you are required to supply an email address in order to register at a site consider 'munging' your address so that it can be read by people but not by a spider (but watch in case this violates your agreement with your ISP). For example:

janeNOSPAMbloggs@isp.com

Alternatively, get an additional email address to use in these situations and keep your main email address for mail that you want to receive.

Web mail

If you want to be able to use email from several locations, or while you are travelling; you might consider opening a web mail account which is accessed through a browser over the World Wide Web. MSN Hotmail is available from Microsoft and is free but your own ISP may also offer a web mail service. Yahoo! also provide free web mail but you will find it possible to collect lots of free email addresses from other sites, should you feel it necessary.

Chapter 9
Security

The least you need to know...

Viruses

A **virus** is just another computer program but if you let one into your computer it will copy itself into your files where it may cause some damage. Most viruses produce only minor problems but the worst examples can delete important files on your hard disk. The key words here are 'if you let one into your computer' because for viruses to spread from computer to computer the virus writer needs to trick you, the user, into helping them on their way.

The most likely ways in which a virus might enter your computer are from a disk that someone has given you or from the Internet.

If a friend hands you a floppy disk to transfer a file to your machine then scan it first with an antivirus program. If your boss gives you a CD-R with a file to work on then scan the disk first with an antivirus program. Don't worry about potentially offending them. Your antivirus program may be more up-to-date then theirs or it might be from a different company – not all antivirus programs catch the same viruses. Always scan floppy disks or CD-Rs that have been in other machines before you open any files on them.

Most viruses are, however, transmitted by email. The virus is usually carried on the email as an attachment and when the user clicks on the attachment to open it the virus is activated. It may then disrupt your machine in some way, copy itself and forward itself to all the contacts in your address book so spreading itself around the Internet.

When you receive an email with an attachment, check the subject line for unusual or unexpected wording. The LoveBug virus had I LOVE YOU in its subject line and millions of people opened it because the email came from someone they knew.

They didn't pause to right click on the email then move the mouse onto View Attachment where they would have seen the filename ended in .VBS. This was a clue that the email had a virus. It is wise to be careful about files which end in .COM, .VBS or .EXE as these are types of program and may indicate that you are dealing with a virus.

However, it doesn't end here – emails without attachments can also contain viruses. Companies that send out advertisements by e-mail often use HTML e-mail which, like a web page, allows them to include images and animations to make the message more eye-catching. Virus writers can exploit this format by including virus code within the HTML message. All you have to do is open the message to release the virus. To reduce the chance of catching viruses in this way, check that the preview page in Outlook Express is switched off. This is important because the preview feature automatically opens your emails for you and if there is a virus embedded... To disable the preview feature, go to View/ Layout and make sure that Preview Pane is unchecked. Service Pack 2 for Windows XP blocks images and HTML by default.

Fig. 9.1 Uncheck the Preview pane in Outlook Express

A further check to make if you think you have received a virus is to scan the email with antivirus software which is up to date. If you keep these points in mind whenever you receive email you will be less likely to get caught out.

Antivirus software

If your first line of defence is your sense of awareness then antivirus software comes a close second. An antivirus package such as Norton AntiVirus or McAfee VirusScan will run in the background checking your hard disk for viruses, automatically scanning files before you open them, and checking email as it arrives in your inbox or leaves your outbox.

The most important thing to remember about antivirus software is that it very, very quickly becomes out of date. An antivirus scanning program works by comparing your files, or any that you receive, against a database of known virus signatures. Even if a database is a few days old it may not have the ability to recognise the latest viruses in circulation. In January 2004, millions of copies of the My Doom virus were circulating within a mere 24 hours of its release.

You can either check for updates manually by going to the Web site of the provider of your antivirus package or configure the software so that it checks for updates automatically whenever you are online.

Antivirus software also provides protection against other forms of malicious software such as worms and Trojans. **Worms** differ from viruses in that they spread across networks automatically without any 'help' from users – often by taking control of a computer's email system. A **Trojan**, or Trojan horse program, usually presents itself as something interesting or useful such as a game or a utility such as a screen saver but which actually turns out to be something nasty. For example, Trojans are used to implant **spyware** programs such **key loggers** which record your keystrokes (including credit card numbers and bank account details) before mailing them to the **hacker** who has attacked you. In the case of the MyDoom virus part of its payload included setting up a 'back door that turns infected machines into spam relay robots.' [Anatomy of a Virus, The Guardian, 05.02.04]

If you go in to a PC World store and look for the security software section you will see one set of shelves lined with red boxes and another with yellow boxes. The red boxes contain the McAfee range of security products from the American company Network Associates while the yellow boxes hold the equivalent Norton products from Symantec.

McAfee VirusScan consists of several programs which work together to protect your computer.

Use **VirusScan** when you want check your entire hard drive for viruses or if you are going to use a floppy disk that has been in someone else's machine. With VirusScan running, just right click on the file and click on Scan for viruses. You will know within seconds whether the file is clean or not.

VirusScan will also check your emails and any attachments for viruses and if you omit to scan that odd-looking file before opening it, VirusScan's on-access scanning feature will check it for you anyway and quarantine the file if it is infected.

VirusScan has an advanced option called **heuristic scanning**. This feature uses a 'rule of thumb' approach to look for viruses. Instead of checking against a database of *known* virus signatures it looks for 'virus-like' characteristics in the files being scanned. A warning that a virus may be present is flashed onscreen if enough of these characteristics are spotted. This can help find **polymorphic viruses** which are able to alter their own code so trying to catch them by checking against a virus signature database becomes pointless.

VirusScan can checks any files that you download when online and stop certain types of malicious program that can download automatically onto your computer when you visit Web sites. **Java applets** and **ActiveX controls** are programs which are used to support animations and multimedia content on Web sites. They can download automatically to your system when you visit a web site and while they can make the Web a more interesting place to explore they can also be used by hackers to deliver malicious code.

With Microsoft's release of Service Pack 2, Internet Exporer now blocks any program that tries to download itself to your computer.

Norton AntiVirus offers largely similar protection as McAfee VirusScan but the names of the features differ. There are also other developers of antivirus software some of which offer free versions of their products. One of such company is Grisoft who supply the AVG AntiVirus from www.grisoft.com.

Firewalls

Firewalls are your next crucial line of defence. You can buy hardware firewalls and software firewalls. Hardware firewalls are usually found on networks. Most stand-alone home computers rely on software firewalls which are generally less expensive – and you can even download free, basic versions of some packages such as ZoneAlarm.

Firewalls stop hackers from getting access to your machine. Windows XP service pack 2 includes a firewall that is switched on by default. One way in which hackers can get access to your PC is to use a program called a **war dialler** which dials up numbers automatically until it finds a computer that answers. A good firewall will 'stealth' your computer so that if it is 'dialled up' nothing happens. An unstealthed PC will sound just like an unanswered phone to a war dialler but a stealthed PC says 'number unobtainable'.

Another hacking technique used is '**network sniffing**' where traffic on the Internet is monitored until a packet is found that reveals your IP address. With broadband you may have an unchanging, or **static**, IP address so once they have found you they 'know your number'.

Before long you may receive a **port scan** which is the hacker looking for a way into your computer. A firewall wall package will check your system for any vulnerabilities such as open ports and block them. A port is an interface between your computer and the outside world and your PC has thousands of them. These ports are not the hardware connections at the back of your PC. They are 'logical' ports used by Internet protocols but each one represents a possible entry point to your computer.

Once an entry point is identified a hacker can use a range of techniques to exploit weaknesses in your system. Using Windows Update regularly to check for patches to such security vulnerabilities is another weapon in your armoury. Windows XP Service Pack 2 is one such update. If your version of XP predates summer 2004 you can download it using Windows Update. There is a direct link to the Windows Update site from the Start button in Windows XP and ME. You can opt to receive automatic updates by going to Control Panel, choosing Automatic Updates and then selecting the relevant option.

Fig. 9.2 Windows update web page

Unprotected computers can be vulnerable to Denial of Service attacks where a hacker sends a flood of IP packets that overwhelm the system under attack and cause it to close down.

A more worrying scenario arises if the hacker installs a Remote Access Trojan (RAT) such as Back Orifice (BO) on your machine. Using this software the hacker can take control of your machine and use it to launch attacks on other machines, or to send spam, or to steal credit card or banking details from your files. The hacker can remove files, delete files or add files to your hard drive. If you don't currently use a firewall, just pause to consider the nature of some of the files that are found on the Internet. Do you really want to be at risk of one day finding them on your machine? A good firewall will block any communications from a Trojan in the event that you are hacked or inadvertently download one.

If you have not yet upgraded Windows XP with Service Pack 2 you will have to switch on the Internet Connection Firewall as folows:

First click on Start, then Control Panel then Network Connections. Next, right click on your Internet connection, then click on Properties then the Advanced tab to show the following dialog box.

Make sure that the 'Protect my computer…' box is ticked and click OK.

Microsoft's original Internet Connection Firewall is a basic firewall. The SP2 version is an improvement but you should also consider a standalone package.

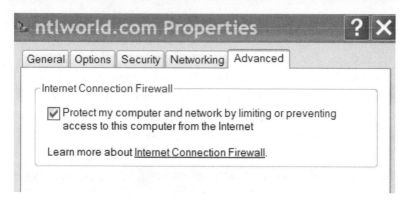

Fig. 9.3 ICF Properties box

McAfee Firewall http://uk.mcafee.com

McAfee's Personal Firewall Plus 2004-5 will:

- Filter software that you trust and block untrusted programs from communicating with the Internet
- Check your computer for possible security vulnerabilities
- Provide intrusion detection to block port scans, denial of service attacks and similar events
- Allow you to block traffic from any IP address
- Give you control over file sharing so that you can block all file sharing when you are on the Internet while on occasions when you want to share files you can see who is accessing your computer

McAfee Firewall is straightforward to set up. Opting for the default settings in the wizard is probably best until you get to know the program better. When you first start using the program you may find that you are presented with a dialog box every time the firewall detects a new program attempting to communicate with the Internet. However, once you have accepted or rejected these options the software just gets on and does its job in the background. There are detailed activity logs if you want to see what has been happening while you were on the Net. The number of warnings that indicate blocked TCP packets coming in from the Internet may surprise you. McAfee Firewall also has a Visual Trace feature which allows you to locate where scans and attacks originated from. However, think twice about using this if you have a fixed IP address as it may reveal your presence to the hacker at the other end.

The ZoneAlarm equivalent of this feature operates from a Zone Labs server which is much safer for the user. The ZoneAlarm Firewall can be downloaded from www.zonclabs.com.

Many developers of software firewalls offer basic versions that can be downloaded for free. However, free versions do not usually allow access to technical support other than user forums and may not be the latest version available. If you want a free-to-use firewall you might want to consider either the free version of ZoneAlarm or the Kerio Personal Firewall which you can find at www.kerio.co.uk.

Hoaxes

Email hoaxes look like genuine emails but may have an attachment when there normally would not be one. For example, if you receive an email that appears to be a security message from Microsoft with an update file attached then please do **not** open it. Microsoft never sends out emails with updates attached – you have to download them from the Web site.

However, you also have to watch out for links to Web sites as well. If an email or a Web site looks even remotely odd or unusual then think twice about clicking on a link. It could be to a spoof site that will then download a program to control your machine. What you can do is go to the actual site by keying in the URL, if you know it, or searching for it via Google. You can then check out if the original message was genuine.

Sometimes hoaxes like this can look very authentic. Microsoft has a good example at :
www.microsoft.com/security/antivirus/authenticate
_mail.asp.

Supplying personal information to Web sites

If you are asked to register at a Web site you usually have to suggest a password. If the site supplies sport results you may not feel too worried about the security of your password but what if you are opening an online bank account? There are three things to consider:

1. Keep passwords secret – if you treat a password as if it were a PIN to your bank account then you will not go far wrong.

2. Make passwords hard to guess. Don't use the first few words of your favourite song or your pet dog's name or your date of birth. Instead, think of a phrase and then randomise it. For example, take the phrase:

Wolf in sheep's clothing

To keep it simple, choose the first letter from each word:

wisc

Now substitute one letter with a number and one with a punctuation character. The letter 'I' looks a bit like an upside down exclamation mark and 'c' is the third letter of the alphabet. Substituting gives:

w!s3

This is not a very long password – the longer the better but hopefully this gives you the idea.

It's a good idea not to use the same password for everything and it can help if you change your password every so often. However, this can make them hard to remember. If you have to note down your passwords, it is best not to put them in a Word file on your machine called 'passwords'!

Privacy statements

If you are going to purchase goods or services from a Website always check whether there is a business address and phone number that you can contact. If you have not done business with them before you might even consider phoning to check things out. Also look for a privacy statement on the Web site and think twice about doing business if there isn't one.

The minimum that you are looking for is a clear statement that they will not sell or 'share' your personal information with third parties – unless they are required to help deliver whatever you are buying.

You should never supply your credit card details to a site that does not provide a Secure Socket Layer (SSL) connection to their server. SSL encrypts the information that is sent between your machine and the server – and it is a lot safer than quoting your credit card number over a phone line. A connection that is protected by SSL will have a window with a URL that begins with https (instead of http). A closed padlock icon will also appear as in the screen below.

Fig. 9.4 Closed padlock icon

If a Web site asks you to provide personal information such as your name, address and phone number over a connection that is not encrypted, then you need to realise that this information will be transmitted from server to server as it makes its way across the Internet and at any one of these locations it could be accessible to a complete stranger. Think twice about providing personal information such as your name, address and phone number to site that is not encrypted.

Internet cafes and libraries are great places to learn about the Internet but it is best to never provide your credit card details to a Web site from a machine that can be accessed by the public. Hackers have been known to load keystroke logging programs onto public machines which then record every keystroke made. The key strokes which may include log-in names, passwords and credit card details can then either be emailed to the hacker or can be picked up from the infected machine at a later date.

Security checklist –10 tips for safer surfing

Use an antivirus program and keep it up-to-date – hundreds of new viruses appear every month.

Use a firewall and go for the best you can afford.

Check regularly for updates to Windows by using the Windows Update link on the Start menu.

Don't open email attachments from strangers and be cautious about opening attachments from people you know.

Always scan any file before opening it – no matter where it came from.

Make passwords hard to guess and keep them secret.

Do not purchase goods or services from a Website that is not prepared to publish a contact address and phone number and think twice about doing business with a site that does not display a privacy policy.

Do not email credit card details and don't provide them

to a site that is not encrypted – look for the padlock icon and make sure the URL begins with https.

Think twice about providing personal information such as your name, address and phone number to a site that is not encrypted.

Never provide your credit card details to a Web site from a machine that can be accessed by the public.

Chapter 10
Accessibility

If you suffer from poor vision, are hard of hearing or have a mobility impairment there are products on the market which are designed to help make computers more accessible for you. There are programs which improve the readability of screens and screen-reading programs can describe toolbars and windows and read text out loud. Voice recognition software can be used to control the operation of the computer and there are even programs which help you with typing by predicting how to complete a word after you have typed the first few characters.

Although Windows cannot offer all the options of a dedicated package for a specific impairment it does provide a number of features to help improve accessibility. If you find it difficult to see text on screen or if using a mouse or operating a keyboard is tricky then you can adjust the settings of these devices through the Control Panel.

Visual

Screen resolution

You can adjust the size at which you view text in programs such as Word and Excel by clicking on View then on Zoom and selecting a magnification that suits you. However, this will not change the size of either menu labels or of icons. One way to see these features at a larger size is to lower your screen resolution.

To adjust screen resolution, click on Start, then point to Settings and click on Control Panel. Locate the Display icon and double click it. Click the Settings tab in the dialog box which appears and move the Screen Resolution slider to a lower setting. This will mean that you will see less onscreen at any one time but everything you can see will be bigger. Click Apply then OK to complete the procedure.

Magnifier

If you find that the slightly increased sizes achieved by adopting a lower screen resolution are not enough, then try Windows Magnifier. Click on Start and point to Programs, then Accessories, then Accessibility, and finally double click on Magnifier. A window opens at the top of your screen in which everything appears magnified.

In the Magnifier Settings dialog box, which also appears, you can set the magnifier to enlarge the part of the screen which you point the mouse to, or if you prefer to use the keyboard to move the cursor around then you can select this option instead.

You can also set the Magnifier to follow the insertion point so that wherever you are editing text the magnifier will show that area enlarged.

The Magnifier provides a range of magnification

levels from 1 (which is of course same size!) to 9. You can increase the size of the magnified pane by clicking and dragging on its bottom edge.

Microsoft describes the Magnifier as providing 'a minimum level of functionality for users with slight visual impairments' – other programs are available that are more appropriate for frequent use.

Narrator

The Windows XP Narrator feature offers an alternative solution for people with impaired vision. You can set Narrator to announce screen events. For example, if Narrator is switched on and you open a window you then hear the name of the window that is being opened followed by a description of the toolbars or buttons available in the window. You can also choose to have every character that you type read allowed.

To open Narrator in Windows XP, click on Start, point to Programs, then Accessories, then Accessibility and click Narrator.

High-contrast colours

If you find it difficult to distinguish between the standard colours that are used by Windows you can select a high-contrast colour scheme from the Accessibility Options in Control Panel. Click on Start, point to Settings then click on Control Panel. Next double click on Accessibility Options, click on the Display tab and select the Use High Contrast option as seen on the next page.

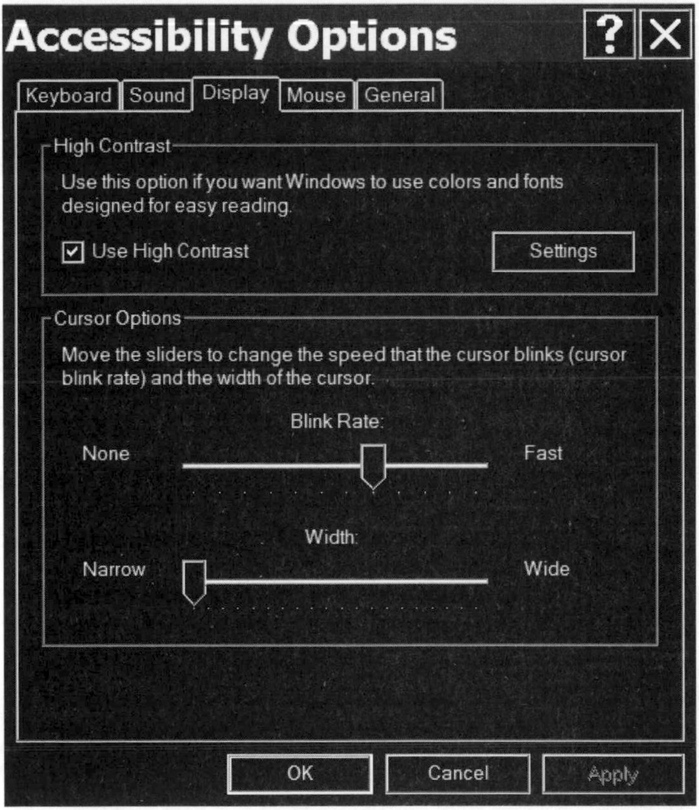

Accessibility Options [?] [X]

| Keyboard | Sound | Display | Mouse | General |

High Contrast

Use this option if you want Windows to use colors and fonts designed for easy reading.

☑ Use High Contrast   [Settings]

Cursor Options

Move the sliders to change the speed that the cursor blinks (cursor blink rate) and the width of the cursor.

Blink Rate:

None ──────────────┬──────────── Fast

Width:

Narrow ──┬──────────────────── Wide

[OK]   [Cancel]   [Apply]

Fig. 10.1 Accessibility Options dialog box with high-contrast switched on

Keyboard

Pressing more than one key at the same time can sometimes be awkward. If you find this difficult, open Control Panel, double click Accessibility Options and click on the keyboard tab. Now select Use StickyKeys. With this feature enabled, you can close a program by pressing Ctrl,

Alt and Delete one after the other – you no longer have to hold down all three keys simultaneously.

The keyboard tab in Accessibility Options also allows you to select FilterKeys. If you press a key and hold it down for a fraction too long Windows interprets this as a request for additional copies of the same character. With FilterKeys enabled Windows will ignore any 'repeated keystrokes' and just give you the single character that you wanted. You can adjust the repeat delay (the time gap between characters repeating when you hold down a key) by clicking on the Settings button and choosing a time which suit you.

The repeat delay can also be adjusted by double clicking on the keyboard icon in Control Panel. If you wish, you can also adjust the repeat rate, which is how quickly characters appear when you depress a key.

Motor difficulties

Mouse

You can adjust your mouse so that the operations of the left and right mouse buttons are reversed. Double click on the mouse icon in Control Panel, select the Buttons tab and select 'Swap left and right button functions...'. From the same dialog box you can slow down (or speed up) your settings for double clicking – which can helpful if you are unable to click the mouse buttons quickly.

If you click on the Pointers tab, which sits next to the Buttons tab in the Mouse Properties dialog box, and then click again on the dropdown menu under Scheme, you can choose larger icons for Windows 'selection tools' such as the arrowhead pointer (normal select) or resize arrows. The next tab along – Pointer options – allows you to adjust how fast the pointer moves across the screen and to display pointer trails if you find that helps improve your view of what is happening onscreen.

Accessibility Wizard

If you find the prospect of adjusting settings through Control Panel a little daunting, then Windows provides an Accessibility Wizard to take you through the various steps. At each stage you can select the options which you would find useful and reject those you do not require.

To open the Accessibility Wizard, click on Start then point to Programs, then Accessories, then Accessibility and finally click on Accessibility Wizard.

Accessibility and Web sites

The Web Accessibility Initiative publishes guidelines for Web site developers to follow which aim to encourage design practices that result in more accessible Web sites. Here are some points to look out for when visiting Web sites.

1. Has the designer provided a text equivalent whenever images are used? Sometimes this may take the form of text which appears as a screentip when the mouse pointer is positioned over an image.

2. Are contrasting colours used to make the text easier to read?

3. Are hyperlinks distinguishable from the rest of the text? For example, are they underlined so that you can see them if you are colour blind? Usability experts such as Jakob Nielsen recommend that unvisited links should appear in blue, active links in red and visited links in purple.

4. Has the designer allowed the user to control the size of onscreen text through their browser? The next time you find a Web site with type which is too small to read, click on View, point to Text Size then click on Largest. On an accessible Web site the text should change size. However, see below for more on this topic.

5. Has an equivalent text-only Web site been provided? If you visit Tesco's Web site using a computer with a monitor set a resolution less than 800 x 600 you are automatically transferred to the tesco.com/access site which is entirely text-based.

6. Can you navigate a Web page easily without using a mouse? Web designers can use an attribute called TABINDEX which allows them to define a tab order so that users who choose not to use the mouse can move through a Web page in a logical manner using the Tab key to select links.

7. Does the Web site feature any of the following logos which indicate that accessibility has been a concern of the developer?

Fig. 10.2 The RNIB, WAI and Bobby logos, see below and page 218

You can make Web sites more viewable by fine-tuning Internet Explorer.

Open Internet Explorer and click on the Tools menu. Click on Internet options and click on the Accessibility button.

You can now choose to 'Ignore font sizes specified on Web pages', 'Ignore font styles specified on Web pages' and 'Ignore colours specified on web pages'. Choose 'Ignore font sizes' and click OK then move to the View menu and point to Text Size then click on Largest.

Further information

The follow links may be of interest if you require more information about an accessibility issue.

http://www.rnib.org.uk/xpedio/groups/public/documents/ code/InternetHome.hcsp

The See it Right logo is awarded to Web sites which meets

the RNIB's Web site standards assessment. There is a list of approved Web sites available on the RNIB site.

http://bobby.watchfire.com/bobby/html/en/index.jsp
Bobby is an organisation which provides a free test site for Web developers to check how accessible their Web sites are.

http://www.w3.org/WAI/
The home page of the Web Accessibility Initiative

http://www.microsoft.com/enable/default.aspx
Microsoft's Accessibility home page has lots of helpful information on from assistive technologies to lists of keyboard shortcuts for all Microsoft programs.

http://www.bbc.co.uk/education/betsie/index.html

Betsie is a program from the BBC which strips out formatting and images from Web pages and re-presents them as text only so that they can be more easily read by screen reading software packages. It works on the BBCi Web site (www.bbc.co.uk) and on some external sites but cannot yet be used across the whole of the Web.

http://www.bbc.co.uk/webwise/

Glossary

ActiveX A type of program that can add interactivity to Web sites.

applications software Software that allows you to carry out what you want to do with the computer such as word processess, send email or surf the Internet.

bit The smallest piece of information that can be stored on a computer. It can either be a 1 or 0.

boot To start or restart a computer

boot loader The program which loads the computer's system software when you switch on your computer.

broadband A fast connection to the Internet; broadband can mean anything from 128 kbps to over 1000 kbps.

browser A program which lets you view web pages.

bug A programming error which prevents a program from working properly or causes the computer to 'freeze' so that nothing works.

byte A group of eight **bits**.

cache Folder where copies of the Web pages that you visit are stored so that the pages load faster the next time that you visit them online.

CD-R Compact Disc-Recordable. A CD that you can 'write' new data on – but just once.

CD-ROM Compact Disc - Read-Only Memory. Storage format similar to an audio CD. The data on a CD-ROM is 'burned' onto it by a laser so that like an audio CD you can access what is on it but you cannot record anything new on it.

CD-RW Compact Disc-Re-Writable. A CD that you can 'write' to more than once.

cookie Small text file that is placed on your hard disk by a Web site. Cookies store information about your computer and which pages you have visited so that the Website can recognise you the next time that you visit.

desktop The first screen that you see once the computer is fully functioning. From the desktop you can start programs and work with files and folders by clicking and dragging the mouse.

dial-up connection Connecting to the Internet via a phone line at speeds of up to 56kbps.

DVD Digital Video Disc. Like an audio CD but with much more storage capacity so that video can be stored (between 4 GB and 17 GB depending on the type of disc).

file Data that is stored in memory and named so that it can be retrieved for use or amendment at a later date.

firewall Either hardware or software to prevent others gaining unauthorised access to your machine when you go online.

flame attack A personal insult posted to a newsgroup or sent by e-mail.

floppy disk Magnetic storage device that, typically, can hold up to 1.4 megabytes of data.

freeware Software where the copyright owner grants you the right to use the program without charge (often for personal use only).

FTP File Transfer Protocol – The rules governing how files are sent across the Internet.

gigabyte Approximately 1000 million bytes of data (see page 00 for explanation). Often abbreviated to GB or referred to as 'Gig'.

gigahertz Unit used to describe the speed of a microprocessor. A chip rated at 1 gigahertz (GHz) can theoretically handle 1 thousand million instructions every second.

Graphical User Interface (GUI) The use of small pictures called icons to represent programs, files or hardware. The programs, files, etc. are accessed by clicking on the icons with the **mouse**.

graphics card A **video adapter** that supports the display of graphics and video. A graphics card usually has its own processor and memory. The faster the processor and the larger the memory, the better the adapter will be at handling video and computer games.

hacker Someone who gains unauthorised access to computers usually for illegal purposes.

hard disk The main storage device for a computer. Usually found inside the computer box but external disk drives are also available.

hardware The equipment such as the screen, the keyboard and the electronic circuits inside the computer box.

HTML Hypertext Markup Language. The language used to format Web pages so that they can be displayed in any **browser.**

hyperlink A link to a related topic which may be on another Web site.

icons Small pictures used to represent programs, files, folders, shortcuts, hardware and system features. See also **graphical user interface.**

inkjet printer Works by spraying ink onto paper through tiny holes in the print 'head'. The 'head' moves back and forth across the page printing one line at a time.

Internet A worldwide network of networks of computers all linked to one another.

ISP Internet Service Provider – company which enables you to connect to the Internet.

kilobyte 1024 bytes of data. Often abbreviated to K.

laser printer A printer that uses photocopier technology to produce a good quality output (300 dots per inch or better).

lurking Reading messages posted to a newsgroup without participating in the discussion.

megabyte Approximately 1 million bytes of data (see page 00 for explanation). Often abbreviated to MB or referred to as 'Meg'.

megahertz Unit used to describe the speed of a microprocessor. A chip rated at 500 megahertz (MHz) can theoretically handle 500 million instructions every second.

meta-search engine Searches other search engines instead of the Web.

microprocessor The 'brain' of the computer. Sometimes referred to as a 'chip' or 'silicon chip', it can process billions of instructions per second and organises the traffic of electronic signals throughout the computer such as directing information to the screen, to the printer or to a disk for storage.

modem (cable) Device that enables you to connect your computer to a cable tv network rather than the telephone network.

modem (dial-up) Device that enables you to connect your computer to a phone line so that you can send and receive emails or surf the World Wide Web. Data can be transferred at speeds of up to 56 kilobits per second (kbs).

mouse Handheld device that enables the user to control the movement of a pointer on the computer screen. The user presses (clicks) the mouse while it is pointing to an onscreen icon or button in order to select from the options available onscreen.

netiquette Etiquette while online.

network sniffing Monitoring Internet traffic for 'packets' which contain IP addresses.

newsgroups Online communities which communicate via electronic discussion boards (Usenet).

operating system See **system software.**

Optical Character Recognition (OCR) Software, used in conjunction with a scanner, to convert text from a printed document so that it can be amended in a word processing program.

peripheral Equipment outside the computer box such as the keyboard, printer, loudspeakers, scanner or joystick for games.

pixel Contraction of 'picture element' – the smallest individual item that can be displayed on a screen.

plug-in A supplementary program. A 'plug in' such as Macromedia's Flash Player enables animations that have been created in Flash to be viewed on websites while browsing with Internet Explorer.

program Instructions which enable the computer to produce something useful.

RAM **R**andom **A**ccess **M**emory is the **main memory** of the computer. It is much faster than disk storage because it has no moving parts but when the computer is switched off anything held in the memory is lost. Modern desktop computers generally have either 256 or 512 megabytes of RAM.

ROM **R**ead **O**nly **M**emory is microprocessor-based memory which unlike RAM does not lose its contents when the computer is switched off. However, you cannot change what is in the memory – it is read-only.

save Transferring the contents of Random Access Memory (RAM) to less volatile memory such as a hard disk.

ScanDisk A utility program which identifies and repairs any errors that occur on your hard disk

scanner Device that converts images into digital form so that they can be stored or altered on a computer.

screen resolution The number of **pixels** that make up the screen image.

search engine A program that looks for keywords in Web pages, newsgroups, etc. and then provides a hyperlink to pages which appear to be relevant.

shareware Software that is free to use without charge for a limited period. At the end of the free period you are asked to send a payment to the author if you intend to continue using the program.

software The instructions or **programs** which control the hardware and allow it to work as a computer

sound card Takes digital signals made up of a stream of 1's and 0's from the CPU and converts them to analogue wave signals for the loudspeakers to then convert into sound. Also works in reverse converting input from a microphone into digital signals that can be handled by the computer.

spam Unsolicited email – often commercially oriented and usually sent to a large number of addresses.

spyware A program which sends information about you to some one else. Marketing companies often use spyware to report back on which websites you visit so that they can build a profile of you for marketing purposes. Usually such information is gathered anonymously and aggregated with other findings so that no single individual can be identified.

system software Software which controls the different parts of hardware which make up the computer system. Also known as the operating system.

TFT Thin Film Transistor – a liquid crystal technology used in the manufacture of flat panel displays. Each **pixel** is a thin film transistor.

toggle To move between opposite states (such as when you switch lights on or off).

touchpad Touch-sensitive panel that together with associated keys performs the function of a **mouse**. Often found in portable computers such as laptop computers.

trackball A pointing device which is in effect an inverted mouse. Useful where work surface space is limited.

trojan A program which usually presents itself as something interesting or useful such as a game or a utility such as a screen saver but which delivers turns out to be malicious

URL Uniform Resource Locator – the technical term for a website address.

utility A program which carries out a very specific task often connected to system management. For example, disk maintenance.

video adapter Part of the computer hardware that handles the signals going to the monitor.

virus A virus is a program which is intended to disrupt the working of other computers.

virus A malicious or nuisance computer program which will copy itself into your files where it may cause some damage. For viruses to spread from computer to computer the virus writer needs to trick the user into assisting the process.

Web log or **blog** Web page that is like an online diary consisting of short items of information and hyperlinks that are arranged chronologically with the most recent posting at the top of the page.

wildcard A character used in place of some of the letters in a word when carrying out a search.

window An onscreen 'frame' that may contain icons, or text or pictures.

worm A malicious program like a virus but which does not require human intervention in order to spread.

WWW World Wide Web – the collective term for all the hyperlinked pages available online. (Clicking a hyperlink takes you to a related topic which may be on another Web site.)